"This series is a tremendous resource for those wanting to study and teach the Bible with an understanding of how the gospel is woven throughout Scripture. Here are gospel-minded pastors and scholars doing gospel business from all the Scriptures. This is a biblical and theological feast preparing God's people to apply the entire Bible to all of life with heart and mind wholly committed to Christ's priorities."

> **BRYAN CHAPELL,** President Emeritus, Covenant Theological Seminary; Senior Pastor, Grace Presbyterian Church, Peoria, Illinois

"Mark Twain may have smiled when he wrote to a friend, 'I didn't have time to write you a short letter, so I wrote you a long letter.' But the truth of Twain's remark remains serious and universal, because well-reasoned, compact writing requires extra time and extra hard work. And this is what we have in the Crossway Bible study series *Knowing the Bible*. The skilled authors and notable editors provide the contours of each book of the Bible as well as the grand theological themes that bind them together as one Book. Here, in a 12-week format, are carefully wrought studies that will ignite the mind and the heart."

> **R. KENT HUGHES,** Senior Pastor Emeritus, College Church, Wheaton, Illinois

"*Knowing the Bible* brings together a gifted team of Bible teachers to produce a high-quality series of study guides. The coordinated focus of these materials is unique: biblical content, provocative questions, systematic theology, practical application, and the gospel story of God's grace presented all the way through Scripture."

> **PHILIP G. RYKEN,** President, Wheaton College

"These *Knowing the Bible* volumes provide a significant and very welcome variation on the general run of inductive Bible studies. This series provides substantial instruction, as well as teaching through the very questions that are asked. *Knowing the Bible* then goes even further by showing how any given text links with the gospel, the whole Bible, and the formation of theology. I heartily endorse this orientation of individual books to the whole Bible and the gospel, and I applaud the demonstration that sound theology was not something invented later by Christians, but is right there in the pages of Scripture."

> **GRAEME L. GOLDSWORTHY,** former lecturer, Moore Theological College; author, *According to Plan*, *Gospel and Kingdom*, *The Gospel in Revelation*, and *Gospel and Wisdom*

"What a gift to earnest, Bible-loving, Bible-searching believers! The organization and structure of the Bible study format presented through the *Knowing the Bible* series is so well conceived. Students of the Word are led to understand the content of passages through perceptive, guided questions, and they are given rich insights and application all along the way in the brief but illuminating sections that conclude each study. What potential growth in depth and breadth of understanding these studies offer! One can only pray that vast numbers of believers will discover more of God and the beauty of his Word through these rich studies."

> **BRUCE A. WARE,** Professor of Christian Theology, The ⌐ Baptist Theological Seminary

KNOWING THE BIBLE

J. I. Packer, Theological Editor
Dane C. Ortlund, Series Editor
Lane T. Dennis, Executive Editor

• • • • • •

Genesis	Psalms	Jonah, Micah, and Nahum	Ephesians
Exodus	Proverbs		Philippians
Leviticus	Ecclesiastes	Haggai, Zechariah, and Malachi	Colossians and Philemon
Numbers	Song of Solomon		
Deuteronomy	Isaiah	Matthew	1–2 Thessalonians
Joshua	Jeremiah	Mark	1–2 Timothy and Titus
Judges	Lamentations, Habakkuk, and Zephaniah	Luke	
Ruth and Esther		John	Hebrews
1–2 Samuel	Ezekiel	Acts	James
1–2 Kings	Daniel	Romans	
1–2 Chronicles	Hosea	1 Corinthians	1–2 Peter and Jude
Ezra and Nehemiah	Joel, Amos, and Obadiah	2 Corinthians	1–3 John
Job		Galatians	Revelation

• • • • • •

J. I. PACKER was the former Board of Governors' Professor of Theology at Regent College (Vancouver, BC). Dr. Packer earned his DPhil at the University of Oxford. He is known and loved worldwide as the author of the best-selling book *Knowing God*, as well as many other titles on theology and the Christian life. He served as the General Editor of the ESV Bible and as the Theological Editor for the *ESV Study Bible*.

LANE T. DENNIS is CEO of Crossway, a not-for-profit publishing ministry. Dr. Dennis earned his PhD from Northwestern University. He is Chair of the ESV Bible Translation Oversight Committee and Executive Editor of the *ESV Study Bible*.

DANE C. ORTLUND (PhD, Wheaton College) serves as senior pastor of Naperville Presbyterian Church in Naperville, Illinois. He is an editor for the Knowing the Bible series and the Short Studies in Biblical Theology series, and is the author of several books, including *Gentle and Lowly: The Heart of Christ for Sinners and Sufferers*.

EXODUS

A 12-WEEK STUDY

Matthew R. Newkirk

CROSSWAY®

WHEATON, ILLINOIS

Knowing the Bible: Exodus, A 12-Week Study

Copyright © 2015 by Crossway

Published by Crossway
  1300 Crescent Street
  Wheaton, Illinois 60187

Some content used in this study guide has been adapted from the *ESV Study Bible*, copyright © 2008 by Crossway, pages 139–208. Used by permission. All rights reserved.

Cover design: Simplicated Studio

First printing 2015

Printed in the United States of America

Trade paperback ISBN: 978-1-4335-4306-7
EPub ISBN: 978-1-4335-4309-8
PDF ISBN: 978-1-4335-4307-4
Mobipocket ISBN: 978-1-4335-4308-1

Crossway is a publishing ministry of Good News Publishers.

VP		30	29	28	27	26	25	24	23
16	15	14	13	12	11	10	9	8	7

TABLE OF CONTENTS

SERIES PREFACE

KNOWING THE BIBLE, as the series title indicates, was created to help readers know and understand the meaning, the message, and the God of the Bible. Each volume in the series consists of 12 units that progressively take the reader through a clear, concise study of that book of the Bible. In this way, any given volume can fruitfully be used in a 12-week format either in group study, such as in a church-based context, or in individual study. Of course, these 12 studies could be completed in fewer or more than 12 weeks, as convenient, depending on the context in which they are used.

Each study unit gives an overview of the text at hand before digging into it with a series of questions for reflection or discussion. The unit then concludes by highlighting the gospel of grace in each passage ("Gospel Glimpses"), identifying whole-Bible themes that occur in the passage ("Whole-Bible Connections"), and pinpointing Christian doctrines that are affirmed in the passage ("Theological Soundings").

The final component to each unit is a section for reflecting on personal and practical implications from the passage at hand. The layout provides space for recording responses to the questions proposed, and we think readers need to do this to get the full benefit of the exercise. The series also includes definitions of key words. These definitions are indicated by a note number in the text and are found at the end of each chapter.

Lastly, for help in understanding the Bible in this deeper way, we urge readers to use the ESV Bible and the *ESV Study Bible*, which are available in various print and digital formats, including online editions at esv.org. The *Knowing the Bible* series is also available online.

May the Lord greatly bless your study as you seek to know him through knowing his Word.

J. I. Packer
Lane T. Dennis

WEEK 1: OVERVIEW

▲

The book of Exodus received its name because it records Israel's departure (Greek *exodos*) from Egypt. The book recounts how God graciously delivered Israel from slavery in Egypt, traces their journey through the wilderness, and describes in detail the covenant[1] God made with them at Mount Sinai. In telling this story, Exodus highlights the supreme faithfulness and mercy of God, and contrasts this with Israel's repetitive grumbling, rebellion, and sin. In so doing, this book presents a condensed picture of the gospel. Simply put, Exodus shows us that God saves sinners.

After showcasing his power and glory in freeing Israel from slavery, God gathers Israel to the foot of Mount Sinai where he communicates his will to them through the law. The instructions of the law include both requirements for how Israel is to live (chs. 20–24) and directives for how God is to be worshiped (chs. 25–31). Although Israel continues to demonstrate idolatrous tendencies, God shows himself to be supremely merciful and faithful (chs. 32–34). The book ends with Israel constructing the tabernacle[2] according to God's specifications, and God descending to dwell with them (chs. 35–40). (For further background, see the *ESV Study Bible*, pages 139–144; also online at esv.org.)

▶ Placing It in the Larger Story

Whereas Genesis records God's promise that Abraham would become a great nation (Gen. 12:2), Exodus describes the fulfillment of that promise (Ex. 1:6–7). Moreover, God's covenant with the patriarchs,[3] in which he promised to give their descendants the land of Canaan (Gen. 15:18; 26:3; 35:12), is the reason God delivers Israel from Egypt (Ex. 2:24).

Although God gives Israel the law and comes to dwell in their midst, ultimately Israel will not be faithful to their covenant with him. Only in Jesus do we find a faithful Israelite who keeps God's law while simultaneously embodying God's presence with his people (John 1:14).

▶ Key Verse

"You yourselves have seen what I did to the Egyptians, and how I bore you on eagles' wings and brought you to myself. Now therefore, if you will indeed obey my voice and keep my covenant, you shall be my treasured possession among all peoples" (Ex. 19:4–5a).

▶ Date and Historical Background

In the Gospels, Jesus quotes Exodus 3:6 and ascribes authorship to Moses (Mark 12:26; Luke 20:37). In Exodus, one verse in particular narrows down when Moses finalized the book. Exodus 16:35 says, "The people of Israel ate the manna forty years, till they came to a habitable land. They ate the manna till they came to the border of the land of Canaan." This verse suggests that Moses did not finalize the book of Exodus until *after* the forty years in the desert, when Israel had reached the border of Canaan. This reveals that the original audience of Exodus was the second generation of Israel, camped on the plains of Moab, waiting to enter the Promised Land.

▶ Outline

I. Exodus from Egypt (1:1–18:27)

    A. Israel in Egypt (1:1–11:10)

        1. Israel's oppression and Moses' early life (1:1–2:25)
        2. Moses' call and preparation (3:1–7:7)
        3. The plagues against Egypt (7:8–11:10)

B. From Egypt to Sinai (12:1–18:27)

  1. Passover and exodus (12:1–13:16)
  2. Deliverance at the Red Sea (13:17–15:21)
  3. Journey to Sinai (15:22–18:27)

II. Covenant at Sinai (19:1–40:38)

A. Covenant law at Sinai (19:1–24:18)

  1. Covenant preparation (19:1–25)
  2. Covenant law (20:1–23:33)
  3. Covenant confirmation (24:1–18)

B. Divine Presence with Israel (25:1–40:38)

  1. Instructions for building the tabernacle (25:1–31:18)
  2. Covenant violation, intercession, and renewal (32:1–34:35)
  3. Construction of the tabernacle (35:1–40:38)

As You Get Started

What is your present understanding of the events in Exodus as they relate to God's plan of salvation? How would you summarize the teaching of the book as a whole?

How do you understand Exodus's contribution to Christian theology? From your current knowledge of Exodus, what does it teach us about God, humanity, sin, salvation, and other doctrines?

What has perplexed you about Exodus? What questions do you hope to see answered through this study of Exodus?

▶ **As You Finish This Unit . . .**

Ask God to open your heart and mind as you begin this study of Exodus. Also, take a few minutes and look back through this first unit of study to see what the Lord may be teaching you—and perhaps to highlight or underline anything that jumps out so you can review it later.

Definitions

[1] **Covenant** – A binding agreement between two parties, typically involving a formal statement of their relationship, a list of stipulations and obligations for both parties, a list of witnesses to the agreement, and a list of curses for unfaithfulness and blessings for faithfulness to the agreement.

[2] **Tabernacle** – The tent where God dwelled on earth and communed with his people as Israel's divine king.

[3] **Patriarchs** – The earliest ancestors of Israel, primarily Abraham, Isaac, and Jacob.

Week 2: Israel's Oppression and Moses' Early Life

Exodus 1:1–2:25

The Place of the Passage

The first two chapters of Exodus set the stage for the rest of the book. As Israel expands into a great nation, fulfilling God's promise to Abraham (Gen 12:2), Pharaoh oppresses them and seeks to curtail their growth. The birth of Moses is presented as the climactic, ironic reversal of Pharaoh's oppressive attempts, hinting that Moses will be a key means by which God will rescue his people. The notice at the end of chapter 2, that "God heard their groaning, and God remembered his covenant with Abraham, with Isaac, and with Jacob" (Ex. 2:24), prepares us to see God act further on his promises to the patriarchs and bring Israel out of Egypt and into the Promised Land.

The Big Picture

Although Pharaoh oppresses Israel, God's promises of Israel's growth and deliverance from Egypt begin to take shape.

> ### Reflection and Discussion

Read through the whole passage for this study, Exodus 1:1–2:25. Then review the shorter passages below and write your answers to the following questions. (For further background, see the *ESV Study Bible*, pages 145–147; also available online at esv.org.)

1. Israel's Multiplication (1:1–7)

In Genesis, God created humanity in his "image" (Gen. 1:26–27), which means that humans were designed to serve as God's royal representatives on earth. In the ancient world, the presence of a king's "image" (usually a statue) represented the reign and authority of that king. God then commanded humanity to "be fruitful and multiply and fill the earth" (v. 28), which shows that they were to represent God's kingship to the ends of the earth. In light of this, what does Exodus 1:7 imply about Israel's purpose as a nation? How does Exodus 19:5–6 elaborate upon this idea?

2. Israel's Oppression (1:8–22)

The theme of Israel "multiplying" continues in Exodus 1:8–22, though now this multiplication occurs in the context of oppression. The Hebrew men are presented here as unstoppably reproductive despite oppressive working conditions (vv. 8–14), and the Hebrew women are unstoppably reproductive due to the midwives' disobedience of Pharaoh's oppressive decree concerning childbirth (vv. 15–22). Given the background of Genesis 1:28 for Exodus 1:7, how might Genesis 3:16–17 shed light on what is going on here?

In this passage we see that God's covenant promises for his people are ironically accomplished in the midst of oppression. What are some other biblical examples of this?

In Exodus 1:16 and 1:22, Pharaoh specifies that each Hebrew "son" (and not simply "boy") must be killed. Read ahead in Exodus 4:22–23. Against whom is Pharaoh setting himself up here in chapter 1? What might this imply about those who oppose the church today?

----

3. Moses' Birth (2:1–10)

The Hebrew word for the "basket" in which Moses is placed (Ex. 2:3) occurs elsewhere in the Old Testament only to describe Noah's "ark" (Genesis 6–9). In what other ways does Noah's life foreshadow Moses' life?

Exodus 1:8–22 presented two ironic reversals of Pharaoh's decrees. What ironies do you see in Exodus 2:5–9? Through this pattern, how is Moses presented in the story of his birth?

13

The name "Moses" seems to be related to the Egyptian word for "son" (e.g., Pharaoh Thut*mose*), but it also sounds like the Hebrew verb meaning "to draw out" (Ex. 2:10). Given Pharaoh's decree in 1:22, what is ironic about this double meaning of Moses' name?

4. Moses' Flight (2:11–25)

Since Moses grew up in Pharaoh's household, away from the slave labor, some Israelites likely viewed him as more Egyptian than Hebrew. However, the text twice refers to Israel as "his people" (Ex. 2:11), and Moses even kills an Egyptian for beating a Hebrew (v. 12). Then, when he arrives in Midian, although the women refer to him as an Egyptian (v. 19), he names his son "Gershom," saying, "I have been a sojourner in a foreign land" (v. 22). Based on these observations, what is this section emphasizing?

In Exodus 2:24–25, God is the subject of four successive verbs ("God heard . . . God remembered . . . God saw . . . and God knew"). Why do you think the text repeats "God" as the subject here? What do you think it means for God to "remember" his covenant with the patriarchs?

Read through the following three sections on *Gospel Glimpses*, *Whole-Bible Connections*, and *Theological Soundings*. Then take time to reflect on the *Personal Implications* these sections may have for your walk with the Lord.

Gospel Glimpses

A MERCY-LOVING GOD. These opening chapters of Exodus mention God in only two places: when the midwives spare the Hebrew boys (1:17–21) and when God hears the Israelites' groaning in their slavery (2:23–25). In the first case, God rewards the midwives for mercifully sparing the Israelite children; in the second case, God mercifully looks upon his people as they groan in their slavery. Although Exodus contains many laws and commands that God will require his people to obey, the book starts off with a focus on God's supremely merciful character. It is only after he has lavished mercy on his people that God gives them commands. This mercy of God is reflected elsewhere in the Old Testament (e.g., in the provisions for forgiveness in Leviticus), but it is most evident in the cross of Jesus. Just as God looked at the plight of Israel in slavery to Egypt and was moved to rescue them, so he saw the plight of our slavery to sin (John 8:34) and rescued us.

UNEARNED RELATIONSHIP. Exodus states that the reason God rescued Israel was his faithfulness to his covenant with Abraham, Isaac, and Jacob (2:24; 6:5). This covenant was founded on God's grace, as Abraham did nothing to earn this special relationship with God. Furthermore, when Israel was suffering in their slavery, it is not clear that they cried out *to God* for help; the text simply says that they "groaned because of their slavery and cried out for help," and that this cry "came up to God" (2:23). This ambiguity further emphasizes God's initiative in coming to their rescue and in establishing a relationship with them. Although neither Abraham nor Israel deserved God's relational commitment, he nevertheless bound himself to them and promised to bless them (Gen. 12:2–3). Similarly, those who come to God through faith in Jesus do nothing to merit this saving relationship; God in his grace always takes the first step in bringing us to himself.

Whole-Bible Connections

FRUITFULNESS AND MULTIPLICATION. At creation, humanity was commissioned to "be fruitful and multiply and fill the earth" (Gen. 1:28). This command was repeated to Noah (Gen. 9:1, 7), and God promised the patriarchs that he would enact this multiplication for them (Gen. 17:1–6; 22:17; 26:4; 28:3–

4). We see this promise fulfilled initially in this passage (Ex. 1:7), but God's law makes it clear that the continual fulfillment of this promise is contingent on the people's obedience (Lev. 26:3, 9; Deut. 7:12–13). As time passes and Israel proves unfaithful, God judges them and sends them into exile;[1] yet hope still remains that in the future God will "bring them back to their fold, and they shall be fruitful and multiply" (Jer. 23:3). The New Testament depicts this promise being fulfilled through the word of God, which is "fruitful" and "multiplies" (Acts 6:7; 12:24; Col. 1:6), bringing salvation to sinners and resulting in the "fruitfulness" of good works and in "multiplication" of the knowledge of God (Col. 1:10).

IRONIC REDEMPTION. This passage presents the birth of Moses—who will be the human instrument of God's salvation of Israel—as the climax of a series of ironic reversals of oppression. This pattern of God ironically bringing redemption through oppression can be traced as far back as the promise of Genesis 3:15, where God declares that the seed of the woman will triumph over the seed of the serpent, but will do so while being oppressed ("he shall bruise your head, and you shall bruise his heel"). This ironic pattern reaches its apex in the cross of Christ, in which salvation unto life is achieved through suffering unto death (2 Cor. 13:4), and it continues as the church grows despite the persecutions brought against her (e.g., Acts 8:3–4; Rev. 12:10–11).

▶ Theological Soundings

CIVIL GOVERNMENT. In Exodus 1:15–21, the midwives disobey Pharaoh's decree to murder the Hebrew children and are blessed by God for doing so. Although Scripture commands us to "be subject to the governing authorities" (Rom. 13:1; see also Titus 3:1; 1 Pet. 2:13–15), and says that "whoever resists the authorities resists what God has appointed" (Rom. 13:2), such subjection is not warranted when the governing authorities command believers to violate God's standards. In Acts 5, when the council of the Sanhedrin interrogates the apostles concerning their violation of the command to stop teaching in Jesus' name, the apostles reply, "We must obey God rather than men" (Acts 5:29).

COVENANT. God is moved to act on Israel's behalf because of the covenant he made with their ancestors (Ex. 2:24–25). In Scripture, covenants are a central means by which God interacts with humanity and brings about his redemption. After Adam broke his covenant with God by disobeying him (see Hos. 6:7), God made a series of covenants with Noah (Gen. 9:8–17), Abraham (Gen. 15:7–20; 17:1–14), Israel (Exodus 19–24), David (Ps. 89:1–4; 2 Sam. 7:8–16), and Jesus (Matt. 26:28; Mark 14:24; Luke 22:20) to restore humanity's fractured relationship with him. Since Jesus is the perfect Mediator[2] of the new covenant (Heb. 12:24), those who come to him in faith are secure in their forgiveness.

Personal Implications

Take time to reflect on the implications of Exodus 1:1–2:25 for your own life today. Make notes below on the personal implications for your walk with the Lord of the (1) *Gospel Glimpses*, (2) *Whole-Bible Connections*, (3) *Theological Soundings*, and (4) this passage as a whole.

1. Gospel Glimpses

2. Whole-Bible Connections

3. Theological Soundings

4. Exodus 1:1–2:25

As You Finish This Unit . . .

Take a moment now to ask for the Lord's blessing and help as you continue in this study of Exodus. And take a moment also to look back through this unit of study, to reflect on some key things that the Lord may be teaching you—and perhaps to highlight and underline these things to review again in the future.

Definitions

[1] **Exile** – A forced resettlement of a population, usually due to military conquest.

[2] **Mediator** – One who intercedes between parties to resolve a conflict or achieve a goal.

Week 3: Moses' Call and Preparation

Exodus 3:1–7:7

The Place of the Passage

Now that the stage is set with Israel in slavery and God poised to act on his covenant promises, this section records God's call and preparation of Moses to lead Israel out of Egypt. Although God repeatedly promises to make good on his word and accompany Moses in leading Israel out of Egypt, both Moses and Israel struggle to believe in the midst of their difficult circumstances. Nevertheless, God assures his people that they will know that he is the Lord when he redeems them and judges Egypt. In the following chapters God will prove himself faithful to this promise by delivering Israel from slavery "with an outstretched arm and with great acts of judgment" (Ex. 6:6).

The Big Picture

God promises to deliver Israel from slavery in Egypt, but the Israelites struggle to believe in the midst of their oppression.

> ### Reflection and Discussion

Read through the whole passage for this study, Exodus 3:1–7:7. Then review the shorter passages below and write your answers to the following questions. (For further background, see the *ESV Study Bible*, pages 147–154; also available online at esv.org.)

1. The Burning Bush (3:1–22)

Exodus 3:1–12 records the theophany[1] of the burning bush, in which God calls Moses to lead Israel. In the broader context of Exodus as a whole, what does the "flame of fire" (3:2) foreshadow? What is therefore special about this location that makes it "holy ground" (3:5)?

In Exodus 3:8 God says that he will "bring [Israel] up out of that land," but then two verses later he tells Moses, "Come, I will send you to Pharaoh that *you* may bring my people, the children of Israel, out of Egypt" (v. 10). What does this reveal about how God carries out his salvation in the world?

God tells Moses that, upon Israel's release, they will "plunder the Egyptians" by receiving silver, gold, and clothing from them (3:22). Plundering was what ancient armies did to cities they conquered in battle. According to vv. 19–21, who is going to do the fighting in this battle? What does this teach us about what it means to be "warriors" in God's army?

2. Moses' Signs and Return to Egypt (4:1–31)

In Exodus 4:1–9, God gives Moses several signs to validate his leadership. How does Moses respond in verse 10? How does God respond to Moses in verses 11–12? From this, what do we learn about the relationship between gifts and faith in serving God?

Before Moses has his first encounter with Pharaoh, God says that he will "harden [Pharaoh's] heart, so that he will not let the people go" (4:21). Why do you think God would do this? How might this push back against common preconceptions concerning how God interacts with people?

21

In Exodus 4:24–26, why is God about to kill Moses (hint: see Gen. 17:12–14)? What does this teach us about those whom God calls to lead?

3. Oppression and Disbelief (5:1–23)

In chapter 5, Moses and Aaron faithfully obey God's word and ask Pharaoh to release the people (vv. 1–3). This results in Pharaoh further oppressing the people (vv. 4–19) and the people condemning Moses and Aaron (vv. 20–21). What does this show us about the potential results of "faithful obedience" to God in a sinful world?

In the ancient world there were "kings" or "suzerains" who ruled, and there were "servants" or "vassals" who were their subjects. A servant could be loyal to only one king. Read Exodus 5:15–16. How do the Israelite foremen view themselves at this point in the story? According to Exodus 4:23, what is the goal of the Israelites' deliverance from Egypt? What might this imply about the goal of our deliverance in Christ?

4. Divine Reassurance (6:1–7:7)

After Moses complains to God about Israel's worsening circumstances (5:22–23), God initially responds not by alleviating their difficulty but by recalling his covenant and reiterating his promises (6:1–8). What do you think God was teaching Israel by doing this? How might this apply to us when we find ourselves in difficult circumstances?

Despite God's reassurances after Moses complains, Israel still does not believe (6:9). Nevertheless, the text repeatedly emphasizes that God continues to command Moses and Aaron to proceed in carrying out his redemption of the people (6:10–13, 26–29; 7:1–2). What does this show us about God's prerequisites for those whom he chooses to save?

Read through the following three sections on *Gospel Glimpses*, *Whole-Bible Connections*, and *Theological Soundings*. Then take time to reflect on the *Personal Implications* these sections may have for your walk with the Lord.

▶ Gospel Glimpses

CHOOSING UNLIKELY LEADERS. In these chapters, Moses is presented as an unlikely leader. He isn't seeking a leadership role (3:1–3), doesn't think he is significant enough for the task (3:11), isn't a good speaker (4:10), tries to get out of the job (4:13), doesn't follow the rules well (4:24–26), and is a complainer (5:22–23). However, God often chooses to work through such people. Jacob was wily, Joseph was a slave, David was the youngest, and the apostle Paul was a persecutor of the church, yet God chose each in their time to lead his people in accomplishing his divine purposes. By choosing such unlikely leaders to carry out his work, God highlights his own grace and power in salvation (see 1 Cor. 15:9–10).

DELIVERANCE FOR DOUBTERS. Despite God's repeated assurances of his personal presence in redeeming his people (3:12; 4:12, 15; 6:1–8), they repeatedly doubt and disbelieve (5:21–23; 6:9). Nevertheless, as the story moves forward,

God's covenant love for Israel moves him to deliver this doubting people anyway (see Deut. 7:7–8). Similarly, though we were once chronic spiritual doubters—indeed, we were "dead in [our] trespasses and sins," totally faithless, as Paul says (Eph. 2:1)—"because of the great love with which he loved us . . . [God] made us alive together with Christ—by grace you have been saved" (Eph. 2:4–5).

▶ Whole-Bible Connections

GOD'S PRESENCE. A repeated theme throughout this section is God's presence. Moses must remove his sandals because God's presence makes the ground holy (3:5). As mentioned above, God repeatedly promises his presence in delivering Israel (3:12; 4:12, 15; 6:1–8), and as discussed below, even God's name reflects his presence with his people. By the end of Exodus, God will dwell with his people through the tabernacle, as he later will through the temple (1 Kings 8:10–11). Although God removed his presence from the temple during the Babylonian exile[2] (Ezek. 11:23), the divine presence returned with Jesus, who "dwelt [lit. "tabernacled"] among us" (John 1:14). After Jesus ascended, he poured out the Holy Spirit, who now makes the church God's temple (1 Cor. 3:16). When Jesus returns and all things are made new, God's presence with humanity will be permanent: "Behold, the dwelling place of God is with man. He will dwell with them, and they will be his people, and God himself will be with them as their God" (Rev. 21:3).

GOD'S NAME. In Exodus 3:13–22, God tells Moses his name, "The LORD," which translates the Hebrew name "*YHWH*" and is related to the verbal phrase "I AM WHO I AM" (v. 14). As the ESV text note says, this phrase may also be translated, "I WILL BE WHAT I WILL BE." Insight into the significance of this name comes from observing that this same verbal phrase ("I will be") occurs just two verses prior, when God assures a doubtful Moses by saying, "I will be *with you*" (3:12). Therefore, contextually, God's name reflects the fact that he will be "with" his people. Centuries later, Isaiah prophesied the virgin birth of a child named "Immanuel" (Isa. 7:14), which means "God with us." Centuries after that, Matthew tells us that this prophecy was fulfilled in the birth of Jesus (Matt. 1:23), whose name means, significantly, "*YHWH* saves" (see Matt. 1:21).

GOD'S SON. The theme of Israel as God's "son" first appears in this section (Ex. 4:22–23). God rescues Israel from slavery the way that a father protects his son. Yet as time goes on, Israel will repeatedly turn away from God and live as a disobedient son. Through the prophet Hosea, God later recalls, "When Israel was a child, I loved him, and out of Egypt I called my son" (Hos. 11:1). However, God goes on to say, "The more they were called, the more they went away" (Hos. 11:2). Eventually this disobedient son would be disciplined through exile, and God would send another Son as a redeemer. When Joseph took Mary and Jesus down to Egypt to avoid Herod's genocide (Matt. 2:14–15), Matthew tells us that this fulfilled Hosea 11:1. That is, Jesus was replaying Israel's role as God's "son" in the exodus. However, as the perfect Son of God, Jesus obeyed where Israel had disobeyed, and because of Jesus' perfect obedience, we who believe in him now receive "adoption as sons" (Gal. 4:4–5).

▶ Theological Soundings

TRANSCENDENCE AND IMMANENCE. Two fundamental attributes of God are his transcendence and his immanence. God's transcendence refers to his complete distinction from and sovereignty over creation. This distinguishes biblical faith from pantheism, which views all of creation as divine. God's immanence refers to his personal presence and involvement in creation. This distinguishes biblical faith from deism, which views God as distant and uninvolved in creation. Both attributes are reflected in this section as the transcendent God sovereignly hardens Pharaoh's heart, while the immanent God draws near to his people as he prepares to deliver them from their bondage.

SOVEREIGNTY OVER UNBELIEF. Twice in this section God says that he will harden Pharaoh's heart so that he will not listen to Moses and release the people (Ex. 4:21; 7:3). Although mysterious to us, in his wisdom God sees fit to use and even facilitate human rebellion and unbelief for his good purposes. In this section, God states that Pharaoh's resistance will provide him the opportunity to showcase his salvation of Israel by bringing judgment upon Egypt (7:4–5). Similarly, the book of Acts reveals that God used the rebellion and unbelief of Herod, Pontius Pilate, and others to showcase the greatest act of salvation ever—the crucifixion of Jesus—all of which God sovereignly "predestined"[3] (Acts 4:27–28).

▶ Personal Implications

Take time to reflect on the implications of Exodus 3:1–7:7 for your own life today. Make notes below on the personal implications for your walk with the Lord of the (1) *Gospel Glimpses*, (2) *Whole-Bible Connections*, (3) *Theological Soundings*, and (4) this passage as a whole.

1. Gospel Glimpses

2. Whole-Bible Connections

3. Theological Soundings

4. Exodus 3:1–7:7

> ## As You Finish This Unit . . .

Take a moment now to ask for the Lord's blessing and help as you continue in this study of Exodus. And take a moment also to look back through this unit of study, to reflect on some key things that the Lord may be teaching you—and perhaps to highlight and underline these things to review again in the future.

Definitions

[1] **Theophany** – An appearance of God to a human being.

[2] **Babylonian exile** – The forced resettlement of Judah out of their land and into Babylon in 586 BC.

[3] **Predestine** – To sovereignly determine beforehand.

WEEK 4: THE PLAGUES AGAINST EGYPT

Exodus 7:8–11:10

▲

The Place of the Passage

Whereas the previous section highlighted God's repeated promises of deliverance and Israel's struggle to believe, in this section God begins to deliver Israel by showcasing his sovereignty over Egypt through the plagues. By repeatedly hardening Pharaoh's heart, God creates an environment in which his gracious salvation of Israel may be fully acknowledged. Ultimately, these chapters depict a power contest between the Lord (represented by Moses and Aaron) and the gods of Egypt (represented by Pharaoh). Although Pharaoh resists and disobeys the divine word, God will eventually overpower him until he submits and releases the people.

The Big Picture

God demonstrates his supremacy over Egypt and his faithfulness to Israel by sending plagues against the Egyptians while protecting Israel from the destructive effects of the plagues.

▶ Reflection and Discussion

Read through the whole passage for this study, Exodus 7:8–11:10. Then review the shorter passages below and write your answers to the following questions. (For further background, see the *ESV Study Bible*, pages 154–162; also available online at esv.org.)

1. Introductory Sign (7:8–13)

In Exodus 7:8–13, in order to validate his and Moses' message before Pharaoh, Aaron casts down his staff so that it becomes a serpent. Earlier this same sign had caused Israel to believe (see 4:1–5, 30–31), but here Pharaoh refuses to listen and believe. What do these different responses reveal about the effectiveness of miraculous signs for bringing about faith?

In ancient Egypt, the serpent was a symbol of Pharaoh's power. What does this introductory section therefore imply about the plagues that will follow?

2. The First Nine Plagues (7:14–10:29)

Exodus 7:14–25 records the first plague, in which the Nile is turned to blood. Here God tells Moses to stand "on the bank of the Nile" and to take with him "the staff that turned into a serpent" (v. 15). Recalling previous passages, what is the combined significance of *Moses* confronting Pharaoh by *the Nile* (see 2:10) and taking this particular staff with him (see 7:8–13)?

Several times throughout the plagues, Pharaoh attempts to bargain with Moses and dictate the terms of his obedience. He offers to allow Israel to sacrifice within the land of Egypt (Ex. 8:25), to allow them to sacrifice but "not go very far away" (8:28), for only the men to go (10:11), and for the people to go without their flocks and herds (10:24). All of these bargains are rejected. What are some ways that we attempt to "bargain" with God when it comes to our obedience?

Although this section is primarily concerned with God's judgments against Pharaoh and Egypt, on several occasions Moses intercedes with God on behalf of Pharaoh (Ex. 8:12, 29; 9:33; 10:18). Why might these intercessions be recorded throughout this section? What do they contribute to this narrative filled with judgment?

According to Exodus 9:14–16, why did God bring these plagues against the Egyptians? What is therefore the ultimate goal of God's judgment of his enemies?

At various points, certain Egyptians recognize God's power throughout the plagues. After the magicians fail to replicate the plague of gnats, they exclaim, "This is the finger of God" (Ex. 8:19). During the plague of hail there are some who "feared the word of the LORD among the servants of Pharaoh" and rush their slaves and livestock inside (9:20). Some of these servants also later implore Pharaoh to release Israel, saying, "Do you not yet understand that Egypt is ruined?" (10:7). In light of Pharaoh's attitude, what do these responses contribute to the story?

3. The Threat of the Tenth Plague (11:1–10)

How is God portrayed as supremely sovereign in Exodus 11:1–3? What does he control? How does this inform our understanding of our own salvation?

In the ancient world, the firstborn was the primary heir of the father's estate. With this background, what are some implications of the tenth plague—the death of all the firstborn in Egypt (11:4–5)—as well as of Israel's being God's "firstborn son" (4:22–23)?

Read through the following three sections on *Gospel Glimpses, Whole-Bible Connections,* and *Theological Soundings.* Then take time to reflect on the *Personal Implications* these sections may have for your walk with the Lord.

▶ Gospel Glimpses

THE WORD OF GOD. These chapters emphasize that the driving force behind the judgment of the plagues is the word of God. Repeatedly we see phrases such as, "the LORD said to Moses" (Ex. 7:14; 8:1, 16, 20; 9:1, 8, 13, 22; 10:1, 12, 21; 11:1), "as the LORD had said/spoken" (7:13, 22; 8:15, 19; 9:12, 35), "as the LORD commanded" (7:10, 20), and "Thus says the LORD" (7:17; 8:1, 20; 9:1, 13; 10:3; 11:4). Just as God's word was the primary means by which he created the world (Genesis 1), so is his word the primary means by which he saves his people through judgment against Egypt. Similarly, the Son of God came to earth as the Word of God (John 1:1), and through him God again brought salvation through judgment. However, in the case of Jesus, he as the Son and Word of God took God's judgment upon himself in order to bring salvation to his people.

CONQUERING OUR ENEMIES. Bound up with God's salvation of Israel was his conquering of their enemies. When the Egyptian magicians mimicked Aaron's initial sign by turning a staff into a serpent, Aaron's staff swallowed theirs (7:12). This event foreshadows the significance of the upcoming plagues: by them God is powerfully conquering Pharaoh and Egypt in order to save his people. Likewise, the gospel of Jesus is not simply the good news that we are saved from the divine wrath that our sins deserve, but also that through Jesus God has inaugurated his kingdom and is conquering all our enemies, the fiercest of which is Satan,[1] the original serpent. In Revelation 12:10, after seeing Satan conquered and cast out of heaven, John hears a loud voice exclaim, "Now the salvation and the power and the kingdom of our God and the authority of his Christ have come, for the accuser of our brothers has been thrown down."

Whole-Bible Connections

CREATION UNDONE. The plagues are depicted as a destructive undoing of the created order in Egypt. The plague of blood on "all their *pools* of water" (Ex. 7:19) corresponds to "the waters that were *gathered* [lit. "*pooled*"] together" to make the seas in creation (Gen. 1:10). The frogs (Ex. 8:1–7) correspond to the "swarms of living creatures" from the waters (Gen. 1:20). The gnats (Ex. 8:16–19) correspond to the "creeping things" on the earth (Gen. 1:24). The flies (Ex. 8:20–24) correspond to the "flying things" (Gen. 1:20, ESV footnote). The livestock (Ex. 9:1–7) corresponds to the "livestock" that Adam named (Gen. 2:20). The hail (Ex. 9:22–26) and locusts (Ex. 10:1–15) together destroyed "all the plants in the land" (Ex. 10:15), corresponding to the "plants" and vegetation of creation (Gen. 1:12). The darkness over Egypt (Ex. 10:21–23) reverses God's first creative act of making light (Gen. 1:3). And finally, the death of the firstborn (Ex. 11:4–5) corresponds to the creation of the first humans (Gen. 1:26). Similarly, the New Testament says that, at the end of time, God will again undo creation in a final act of judgment, after which he will re-create the world in righteousness (2 Pet. 3:10–13).

HARDNESS OF HEART. Throughout the plague narrative, Pharaoh's heart is unswervingly hard. It is variously stated that Pharaoh's heart "was/is hardened" (Ex. 7:13, 14; 8:19; 9:7, 35), that Pharaoh "hardened his heart" (8:15, 32; 9:34), and that God hardened Pharaoh's heart (9:12; 10:1, 20, 27; 11:10). This hard-heartedness prevents Pharaoh from obeying God's word and releasing Israel, and therefore results in his just judgment. Psalm 95:8–11 notes that this exodus generation of Israel also hardens their hearts after leaving Egypt, which similarly results in their not obeying God's word and thus receiving God's judgment. The psalmist takes this opportunity to exhort his readers not to harden their hearts as that generation did, an exhortation that the writer of Hebrews picks up and applies to his Christian audience, encouraging them to hold fast to Christ: "For we have come to share in Christ, if indeed we hold our original confidence firm to the end. As it is said, 'Today, if you hear his voice, do not harden your hearts as in the rebellion'" (Heb. 3:14–15).

Theological Soundings

HOLINESS. To be "holy" means to be set apart, and although the word "holy" does not occur in these chapters, these stories show again and again that Israel was set apart for God. While addressing Pharaoh, God repeatedly refers to Israel as "my people" who are to be released (Ex. 7:16; 8:1, 20, 21, 22, 23; 9:1, 13, 17; 10:3), while Egypt is "your people" who will suffer the judgment of the plagues (8:3, 4, 9, 11, 21, 23; 9:14, 15). Further, as the plagues go on, Israel is increasingly set apart from the Egyptians. By the third plague the magicians are no longer able to replicate Moses and Aaron's signs (8:18; 9:11), and beginning with the fourth plague the land of Goshen is set apart and protected from the devastating effects of the plagues (8:22; 9:26). Widening our scope, we can see that Israel's salvation stems out of God's own holiness (3:5) and will result in their being established as God's "holy nation" (19:6).

ELECTION. The doctrine of election states that God sovereignly chooses whom he will save and whom he will not. As Paul notes, this doctrine is evident in God's choosing Isaac over Ishmael (Rom. 9:6–7) and Jacob over Esau (vv. 10–12). However, Paul's argument for election reaches its climax by recalling God's hardening and rejection of Pharaoh: "For the Scripture says to Pharaoh, 'For this very purpose I have raised you up, that I might show my power in you, and that my name might be proclaimed in all the earth.' So then he has mercy on whomever he wills, and he hardens whomever he wills" (Rom. 9:17–18; see Ex. 9:16). Pharaoh therefore serves as an example of one whom God has not elected unto salvation.

> ## Personal Implications

Take time to reflect on the implications of Exodus 7:8–11:10 for your own life today. Make notes below on the personal implications for your walk with the Lord of the (1) *Gospel Glimpses*, (2) *Whole-Bible Connections*, (3) *Theological Soundings*, and (4) this passage as a whole.

1. Gospel Glimpses

2. Whole-Bible Connections

3. Theological Soundings

4. Exodus 7:8–11:10

> ### As You Finish This Unit . . .

Take a moment now to ask for the Lord's blessing and help as you continue in this study of Exodus. And take a moment also to look back through this unit of study, to reflect on some key things that the Lord may be teaching you—and perhaps to highlight and underline these things to review again in the future.

Definitions

[1] **Satan** – A spiritual being whose name means "accuser." As the leader of all the demonic forces, he opposes God's rule and seeks to harm God's people and accuse them of wrongdoing.

WEEK 5: PASSOVER AND EXODUS

Exodus 12:1–13:16

▲

These chapters record the climactic finale of God's plagues against the Egyptians, in which the death of every firstborn in Egypt moves Pharaoh to release the Israelites from bondage. As God brings judgment against Egypt, he gives Moses instructions for the Passover sacrifice so that the plague of death "passes over" the Israelite households. To commemorate this saving event, God instructs the Israelites to keep the Passover and the Feast of Unleavened Bread annually, and to set apart for the Lord every firstborn male. By doing so, Israel was to keep the memory of God's gracious salvation alive throughout their generations.

The Big Picture

God brings his final plague against Egypt by killing every firstborn male, but spares the Israelites who are covered by the blood of the Passover lamb.

▶ Reflection and Discussion

Read through the whole passage for this study, Exodus 12:1–13:16. Then review the shorter passages below and write your answers to the following questions. (For further background, see the *ESV Study Bible*, pages 162–166; also available online at esv.org.)

1. Instructions for the Passover and Feast of Unleavened Bread (12:1–28)

This section starts off by rearranging Israel's calendar around this deliverance from Egypt (12:1–2). What benefits would this have for future generations of Israelites?

Verses 3–13 contain a series of instructions for Israel to follow in preparing the Passover lamb. Why do you think God didn't simply pass over the Israelite houses automatically? What do these instructions reveal about the way God extends salvation to his people?

What are some similarities between the Passover sacrifice and Jesus' sacrifice? For clarification read John 19:36 (comparing Ex. 12:46) and 1 Peter 1:18–19.

Verses 14–20 of Exodus 12 provide instructions for the annual Feast of Unleavened Bread. During this time the Israelites were not permitted to use leaven in their bread, which reflected the haste with which they had to depart Egypt (12:33–34, 39). The Passover meal was similarly to be eaten in haste, with the people dressed for departure, to reenact the sudden Israelite exodus (v. 11). Why was it important for Israel to remember and reenact this event? What are some ways that we in the church remember and reenact our past?

2. Final Plague and Exodus (12:29–42)

When Israel leaves Egypt, the Egyptians give them silver and gold jewelry, which the text interprets as Israel "plundering" the Egyptians (12:35–36). Furthermore, in verse 41 the text refers to the departed Israelites as "all the hosts of the LORD." Both of these are military phrases, portraying Israel as conquering the Egyptians in battle. In light of Exodus 1:10, what is ironic about all this militaristic description?

3. Institution of the Passover (12:43–51)

These verses tell us how the Passover celebration began. Read John 19:36 in conjunction with Exodus 12:46 and Psalm 34:20. How does Jesus ultimately fulfill the Passover?

4. Instructions for Consecrating the Firstborn and the Feast of Unleavened Bread (13:1–16)

Exodus 13:3–10 reiterates further instructions concerning the Feast of Unleavened Bread. Notice how an Israelite is to explain the rationale for keeping this feast (vv. 8–9). Were the particulars of this feast to be kept *in order to* enjoy a relationship with God, or *because* God had already brought about a relationship with Israel through his saving grace? How might this affect how we view the relationship between our salvation and the good works to which God calls us?

Exodus 13:11–13 says that all firstborn males in Israel were to be set apart for God. This meant that either they were to be sacrificed (certain animals) or they were to receive a sacrificial substitution (all male children, certain other animals). What would such a substitution remind an Israelite of? What does this substitution point forward to?

Twice this section looks forward to the future, when Israel will live in the land of Canaan (13:5, 11). In what ways do these verses emphasize God's faithfulness and grace?

Read through the following three sections on *Gospel Glimpses*, *Whole-Bible Connections*, and *Theological Soundings*. Then take time to reflect on the *Personal Implications* these sections may have for your walk with the Lord.

Gospel Glimpses

THE PASSOVER LAMB. The sacrifice of the Passover is one of the clearest pictures of the gospel in the Old Testament. The Israelites were to sacrifice a spotless lamb and smear its blood on their doorframes. When God brought his judgment of death against the land of Egypt, he would see the blood of the lamb and "pass over" the Israelites' houses (Ex. 12:13). Building off this image, the New Testament presents Jesus as "the Lamb of God, who takes away the sin of the world" (John 1:29). Just as the shed blood of the Passover lamb covered the people of Israel so that God's judgment passed over them, so does Jesus' shed blood bring forgiveness to those who put their faith in him (Eph. 1:7). Therefore it is very fitting that the Gospels record Jesus' sacrificial death as occurring during the Passover festival (Matt. 26:2; Mark 14:1; Luke 22:15), making him the fulfillment of this Old Testament ritual. In fact, this association is so strong that Paul actually identifies Jesus as "our Passover lamb" (1 Cor. 5:7).

A MIXED MULTITUDE. Exodus 12:38 notes that when the Israelites left Egypt, "a mixed multitude also went up with them." This indicates that people of other nationalities accompanied the Hebrews as they departed their land of slavery. This short note reflects the fact that God's plan of salvation has always been international in nature. When God called Abram, Israel's ancestor, he told him, "in you all the families of the earth shall be blessed" (Gen. 12:3). Later, when Israel first enters Canaan in their conquest of the Promised Land, Rahab defects from the Canaanites and aligns herself with the Israelites (Joshua 2). This theme reappears, with people such as Ruth the Moabite and Uriah the Hittite showing faith in God, but it is most evident in the New Testament mandate for the gospel to go out to all the nations. Not only does Jesus commission his followers to go out and "make disciples of all nations" (Matt. 28:19), but Paul explains that this good news for the nations was actually contained in God's original promise to Abram back in Genesis 12:3 (Gal. 3:8).

Whole-Bible Connections

SALVATION THROUGH JUDGMENT. A pattern that reappears throughout Scripture is God saving his people through judgment. While the flood brought judgment upon the whole human race during Noah's day, it simultaneously lifted up the ark, saving Noah and his family (Genesis 6–9). Here in the exodus, God's tenth plague of judgment against Egypt also served as the catalyst for Pharaoh to release Israel (Ex. 12:29–32). Later, the prophets will often speak of Israel's salvation from exile by proclaiming judgment against their enemies (e.g., Jer. 46:27–28; Ezek. 28:25–26). The cross of Christ is the most significant example of salvation through judgment: because Jesus was wounded in our place for our transgressions, we are healed (Isa. 53:5; 1 Pet. 2:24). Similarly, at the end of time, God will finalize our salvation by remaking all creation into "new heavens and a new earth" (2 Pet. 3:13), yet he will do so by bringing fiery judgment upon the current creation (2 Pet. 3:7).

GRACE-DRIVEN OBEDIENCE. Three different times in these chapters the Israelites are instructed how to communicate to their children the significance of the rituals described here. In each case, obedience in carrying out the ritual is grounded in the grace of God's salvation. The Passover was to be "observed" as a "statute" (Ex. 12:24) because the Lord "passed over the houses of the people of Israel in Egypt" (12:27). Concerning the "statute" of the Feast of Unleavened Bread (13:10), an Israelite was to say, "It is because of what the LORD did for me when I came out of Egypt" (13:8). Similarly, the practice of devoting the first-born reflected God's deliverance of Israel: "By a strong hand the LORD brought us out of Egypt, from the house of slavery" (13:14). This pattern parallels the relationship of grace and good works in the New Testament. As Paul says, it is by grace we have been saved through faith, and through this gracious salvation we have been "created in Christ Jesus for good works" (Eph. 2:8–10). Therefore, in both the Old and New Testaments, God's grace is the fuel that drives the believer's obedient response.

Theological Soundings

SUBSTITUTION. Central to the gospel message is the glorious truth that Jesus suffered and died on the cross in our place as our substitute. As John says, Jesus "laid down his life for us" (1 John 3:16). This doctrine of substitution is reflected at various points throughout the Old Testament, from the ram that God provided Abraham to sacrifice instead of his son Isaac (Gen. 22:13) to the servant who suffers on Israel's behalf in the book of Isaiah (Isa. 53:4–6). This concept of substitutionary sacrifice is also seen here in the exodus account as the Passover lamb is killed instead of Israel's firstborn males. By providing substitutes, God graciously spares his people from experiencing his judgment.

SACRAMENT. Sacraments are signs established by God that represent his saving work and encourage the faith of believers. Traditionally, Protestants have observed two sacraments: baptism and the Lord's Supper.[1] These New

Testament sacraments provide tangible pictures of the salvation that Jesus has achieved for us. As Paul says concerning the Lord's Supper, "as often as you eat this bread and drink the cup, you proclaim the Lord's death until he comes" (1 Cor. 11:26). As the precursor to the Lord's Supper, the Passover was an Old Testament sacrament that also signified God's saving work. In this passage, God repeatedly instructs the Israelites to observe the Passover and the Feast of Unleavened Bread for generations to come in order to commemorate his saving grace through the exodus (Ex. 12:14, 17, 24–25, 42).

Personal Implications

Take time to reflect on the implications of Exodus 12:1–13:16 for your own life today. Make notes below on the personal implications for your walk with the Lord of the (1) *Gospel Glimpses*, (2) *Whole-Bible Connections*, (3) *Theological Soundings*, and (4) this passage as a whole.

1. Gospel Glimpses

2. Whole-Bible Connections

3. Theological Soundings

4. Exodus 12:1–13:16

▶ As You Finish This Unit . . .

Take a moment now to ask for the Lord's blessing and help as you continue in this study of Exodus. And take a moment also to look back through this unit of study, to reflect on some key things that the Lord may be teaching you—and perhaps to highlight and underline these things to review again in the future.

Definitions

[1] **The Lord's Supper** – A meal of remembrance instituted by Jesus at the Last Supper on the night of his betrayal. Christians are to observe this meal, also called Communion, in remembrance of Jesus' death.

WEEK 6: DELIVERANCE AT THE RED SEA

Exodus 13:17–15:21

▲

The Place of the Passage

In these chapters God fulfills his promises of deliverance by bringing Israel out of Egypt, leading them along the edge of the wilderness, miraculously parting the Red Sea so they can pass through on dry ground, and then bringing the waters back down upon the approaching Egyptian army. This deliverance at the Red Sea is recalled throughout the Old Testament as the paradigmatic account of God's saving work (see, e.g., Neh. 9:11; Ps. 78:13; 136:13–15; Isa. 11:10–16) and opens the door for God to communicate his will to Israel as he brings them to Mount Sinai.

The Big Picture

God leads Israel out of Egypt, saves them by parting the Red Sea, and judges Egypt by bringing the sea back upon them.

▶ **Reflection and Discussion**

Read through the whole passage for this study, Exodus 13:17–15:21. Then review the shorter passages below and write your answers to the following questions. (For further background, see the *ESV Study Bible*, pages 166–169; also available online at esv.org.)

1. Pillars of Cloud and Fire (13:17–22)

As Israel departs Egypt, Moses takes Joseph's bones with them, fulfilling Joseph's final request to his brothers (Ex. 13:19; see Gen. 50:24–25). Why would Joseph want his bones to be transported like this (for help, see Heb. 11:22)? What does this fulfillment of their transport here in Exodus show us about God? How might this have encouraged the original audience of Exodus? (For information concerning Exodus's original audience, review Week 1, "Date and Historical Background.")

2. Crossing the Red Sea (14:1–31)

The chariot was an advanced and formidable military device in the ancient world. Exodus 14:5–9 describes Pharaoh's pursuit of Israel and focuses on his impressive chariot force, mentioning chariots four times in these five verses, and twice noting that "all" of Pharaoh's chariots went after Israel (vv. 7, 9). In light of what God says in verse 4, what effect might this focus on Pharaoh's grand chariot force have had on the original readers of Exodus? How do verses 23–28 reinforce this?

The stated purpose of Israel's deliverance throughout the preceding chapters was that they might "serve" the Lord (e.g., 4:23; 7:16; 8:1, 20; 9:1, 13; 10:3, 7, 8, 11, 24). However, in Exodus 14:11–12 the Israelites highlight their past and present desire to "serve" the Egyptians rather than trust God and follow Moses. What does this suggest about God's spiritual requirements for those whom he saves? How does this highlight God's grace in salvation?

How would you summarize Moses' response to the people's fears in Exodus 14:13–14? What does this indicate is the proper response to God's gracious salvation?

We noted that, throughout the plague narrative, God repeatedly hardened Pharaoh's heart so that he refused to release Israel. Here we see God further hardening the heart of Pharaoh (14:4, 8) and of the Egyptians (14:17). According to these verses, what does this hardening lead Pharaoh and the Egyptians to do? What effect does this hardening ultimately have for God (see vv. 4, 17)?

Verses 22 and 29 of Exodus 14 are nearly identical to each other, which is a literary device used to focus attention on what comes between them. What do verses 23–28 emphasize? How does this emphasis differ from what we might assume the account of the Red Sea focuses on?

3. The Song of Moses (15:1–21)

Supporting the previous observation, the majority of Israel's song of praise recalls God's destructive judgment against Israel's enemies (15:1–12), as does the reprise of verse 21. How might we apply this emphasis to our understanding of our own salvation? For clarification, see Eph. 6:10–13.

After recalling God's judgment of Egypt in Exodus 15:1–12, verses 13–17 describe how this judgment will cause the peoples in and around Canaan to have a fearful recognition of God's power, which will enable Israel to enter the Promised Land. In short, God's faithfulness in the past is presented as grounds for God's people to trust him concerning the future. What does this look like for the Christian?

After describing Israel's future entry into the Promised Land (15:13–17), the song ends by proclaiming God's everlasting kingship (15:18). Why might the song connect these two themes? What does this suggest about the nature of God's kingship?

Read through the following three sections on *Gospel Glimpses, Whole-Bible Connections*, and *Theological Soundings*. Then take time to reflect on the *Personal Implications* these sections may have for your walk with the Lord.

▶ Gospel Glimpses

FAITHFUL TO THE FAITHLESS. When God delivers Israel, he doesn't wait for them to believe before he saves them. Despite their fearful disbelief, he saves them by his grace, which causes them to believe. As the Egyptians approached Israel at the sea, the Israelites "feared greatly" (Ex. 14:10) and showed their unbelief by rebuking Moses for bringing them out of Egypt (14:11–12). Nevertheless, God saved them by bringing them through the Red Sea and sweeping the Egyptians away, after which "the people feared the LORD, and they believed in the LORD" (14:31). Similarly, Jesus accomplished his saving work on the cross for us while we were still unbelievers. As Paul says, "while we were still sinners, Christ died for us" (Rom. 5:8).

KINGDOM OF GOD. Israel's song of praise exalting God for his salvation ends by saying, "The LORD will reign forever and ever" (Ex. 15:18). In creation, God had sought to establish his reign on earth with humanity as his royal representatives (Gen. 1:28), but Adam and Eve sinned and rejected God's kingship. Although the Old Testament affirms that the Lord reigns as king (e.g., 1 Chron. 16:31; Ps. 93:1; 96:10; 97:1; 99:1), throughout this period God's kingdom is not represented well on earth, due to Israel's unrepented sin. However, the New Testament proclaims the good news concerning Jesus, which is repeatedly described as the "good news/gospel *of the kingdom*" (Matt. 4:23; 9:35; Luke 4:43; 8:1; 16:16; Acts 8:12; see also Mark 1:15; Luke 9:2, 11, 60; 10:9; Acts 1:3; 19:8; 28:23, 31). That is, through Jesus, God has redeemed his people and has begun to rule over them as their king. One day, Jesus' reign will fulfill Israel's ancient song of praise: "The kingdom of the world has become the kingdom of our Lord and of his Christ, and he shall reign forever and ever" (Rev. 11:15).

Whole-Bible Connections

PASSING THROUGH THE WATERS. The means by which God saves Israel is having them pass through the waters of the Red Sea. This theme of passing through water recurs at several points throughout the Bible. As Israel enters the Promised Land, when the priests carrying the ark step into the Jordan River, it stops flowing so the people can cross on dry ground (Josh. 3:13–17). Similarly, just before Elijah is taken to heaven in a chariot of fire, he and Elisha separate the waters of the Jordan and pass through on dry ground (2 Kings 2:8–15). Matthew records Jesus replaying Israel's early history, first going down to Egypt (Matt. 2:13–15) and then passing through the waters of the Jordan in baptism (Matt. 3:13–17), which seems to correspond to Israel's Red Sea crossing. Followers of Jesus likewise pass through the waters of baptism to identify with his death and mark our covenant relationship with him. Paul authenticates this description of baptism as "passing through the waters" by saying that Israel was "baptized into Moses" at the Red Sea (1 Cor. 10:2).

THE DIVINE WARRIOR. The theme of God as the divine warrior is prominent in this passage, with both Moses (Ex. 14:14) and the Egyptians (14:25) recognizing that God is fighting on Israel's behalf. This theme reaches its climax in the song at the sea in chapter 15, where the Israelites declare, "The LORD is a man of war; the LORD is his name" (15:3). The Old Testament goes on to portray God as the divine warrior in Israel's conquest of Canaan (Deut. 20:4; Josh. 10:14), in his defense against Israel's enemies during their time in the Promised Land (e.g., 1 Sam. 7:10–12; 2 Chron. 32:21), and in prophetic visions of end-time restoration (Zech. 14:3). Similarly, the New Testament presents Jesus as the divine warrior, triumphing over the spiritual forces of darkness on the cross (Col. 2:15) and empowering the church to engage in spiritual warfare (2 Cor. 10:3–6). At his second coming, Jesus will return to earth as the divine warrior, bringing full salvation to his people by bringing final judgment on his enemies (Rev. 19:11–21).

Theological Soundings

ACCOMMODATION. The doctrine of accommodation states that God communicates to us in ways that accommodate or take account of our frailty and finitude. The reformer John Calvin described it as God speaking to us with "lisps," the way that a nurse speaks to a baby. In so doing, God lowers himself to interact with us in ways that we can handle. In Exodus 13:17–18, as God leads Israel out of Egypt, he doesn't take them directly to Canaan. That would have sent them through Philistine territory, and God knew that such a war-ridden path would make the people fearful and they would want to return to Egypt. Instead, he accommodates their fears and takes them the long way through the wilderness. This illustrates how the God of Scripture is both mighty to save and yet compassionate and attentive to our limitations.

GLORY. God declares that by his hardening and judgment of Pharaoh and the Egyptian army he will bring himself glory (Ex. 14:4, 17–18), and after being saved Israel praises him for "triumph[ing] gloriously" (15:1) and being "awesome in glorious deeds" (15:11). Indeed, God's glory can well be described as the purpose of human existence, as people are created for his glory (Isa. 43:7) and are called to bring him glory in all their activities (1 Cor. 10:31).

POWER. God's salvation of Israel in these chapters is presented as a demonstration of his power. After being delivered, Israel recognizes the "great power" that God used to save them (Ex. 14:31) and so their song of praise that follows is full of descriptions of God's strength and might in salvation (see especially 15:2, 6–17). This emphasis reflects the attribute of God known as omnipotence, which means that he is all-powerful; nothing is too hard for him (Jer. 32:17).

▶ Personal Implications

Take time to reflect on the implications of Exodus 13:17–15:21 for your own life today. Make notes below on the personal implications for your walk with the Lord of the (1) *Gospel Glimpses*, (2) *Whole-Bible Connections*, (3) *Theological Soundings*, and (4) this passage as a whole.

1. Gospel Glimpses

2. Whole-Bible Connections

3. Theological Soundings

4. Exodus 13:17–15:21

> ### As You Finish This Unit . . .

Take a moment now to ask for the Lord's blessing and help as you continue in this study of Exodus. And take a moment also to look back through this unit of study, to reflect on some key things that the Lord may be teaching you—and perhaps to highlight and underline these things to review again in the future.

WEEK 7: JOURNEY TO SINAI

Exodus 15:22–18:27

▲

The Place of the Passage

After God demonstrates his great power through the plagues and finalizes Israel's deliverance at the Red Sea, these chapters record Israel's travels from the Red Sea to the foot of Mount Sinai. Throughout this section Israel is depicted as faithless and grumbling, yet God still provides for all their needs. He provides for their physical need of sustenance on multiple occasions (Ex. 15:22–17:7) as well as their spiritual need for leadership in the face of both external (17:8–16) and internal (18:1–27) problems. Ultimately, God sustains his people as he brings them to his mountain (18:5) in order to confirm his covenant relationship with them.

The Big Picture

On the journey from the Red Sea to Mount Sinai, the Israelites repeatedly reveal their lack of faith, yet God continues to show himself faithful by providing for them.

► Reflection and Discussion

Read through the whole passage for this study, Exodus 15:22–18:27. Then review the shorter passages below and write your answers to the following questions. (For further background, see the *ESV Study Bible*, pages 170–174; also available online at esv.org.)

1. God's Provision of Sustenance (15:22–17:7)

Immediately after God delivers Israel through divided water, Israel grumbles that they have no drinkable water (15:22–24). However, based on God's deliverance at the Red Sea, Israel should have responded to this seemingly dire circumstance by trusting God rather than grumbling. What does this pattern (i.e., deliverance leads to trust despite dire circumstances) look like for a Christian?

The opening verses of the manna episode (Ex. 16:1–5) contain elements of sin, grace, and law. Identify each of these elements in these verses. Of the latter two, which comes first, grace or law? Why is this significant?

Twice in Exodus 16:6–8, Moses interprets the people's grumbling against him and Aaron as grumbling against God. What does this suggest about the nature of Moses' leadership over Israel? How does this then inform our understanding of the people's actions in 16:19–20?

In Exodus 16:16–26, God gives the people instructions for how to gather the manna. They are to gather just enough for each day's consumption, and enough on the sixth day for two days' consumption. According to Moses' later interpretation of this in Deuteronomy 8:2–3, what were these instructions supposed to teach Israel?

At first glance, Exodus 17:1–7 seems to be about Israel grumbling for water again. However, verse 7 suggests that a deeper sin problem is the issue here. What is this problem? What are we to learn from this (see 1 Cor. 10:1–6)?

2. God's Provision of Leadership (17:8–18:27)

Israel's battle against Amalek contains the last appearance of the "staff of God" (17:9), which was the instrument used to bring the plagues against Egypt (e.g., 4:17, 20; 7:17; 8:5, 16; 9:23), to part the Red Sea (14:16), and to bring water from the rock (17:5). What do these prior uses of the staff suggest about the nature of the battle that ensues?

At the Red Sea, God fought Egypt *for* Israel (14:14). At Rephidim, however, God fights Amalek *through* Israel (17:8–16). What might these two types of physical warfare illustrate for us concerning God's role and our role in the spiritual battles we face today?

The last time Jethro and Zipporah were mentioned was in chapter 4, just before Moses returned to Egypt to begin the exodus (Ex. 4:18–25). Why might the writer emphasize their presence here at the beginning of chapter 18? (Note that Moses' "father-in-law" is mentioned eight times in the first 12 verses [Ex. 18:1, 2, 5, 6, 7, 8, 12 (2x)].)

The narratives of Exodus 15:22–17:7 portray Israel as generally faithless, despite being delivered by God from Egypt. What is ironic about the response of Jethro—who is reintroduced in 18:1 as "the priest of Midian"—to this same event (Ex. 18:8–12)? For further insight, see Matthew 3:7–9; Romans 2:28–29; Galatians 3:7.

In Exodus 18:13–22, Jethro gives Moses advice for how to assign leadership responsibilities over Israel. According to verse 23, what ultimately undergirds the success of Moses' leadership strategy? What does this imply for leaders of God's people today?

Read through the following three sections on *Gospel Glimpses*, *Whole-Bible Connections*, and *Theological Soundings*. Then take time to reflect on the *Personal Implications* these sections may have for your walk with the Lord.

▶ Gospel Glimpses

BREAD FROM HEAVEN. Not long after expressing fear over the approaching Egyptian army and experiencing God's powerful salvation (Exodus 14), the Israelites grumble that they have no food (16:2–3). As he did previously, here again God graciously responds to their concerns and declares that he will "rain bread from heaven for you" (16:4). God provided this heavenly bread— manna—for the entirety of Israel's wilderness wandering to sustain them throughout their travels (16:35). Similarly, when Jesus was faced with 5,000 hungry followers, he also fed them with miraculous bread (John 6:1–14). He then went on to identify himself as the living bread that has come down from heaven (v. 51). Jesus notes that though Israel was sustained by the manna in the wilderness, eventually they all died. However, those who feed upon Jesus, the living bread from heaven, will live forever (v. 58).

WATER FROM THE ROCK. Immediately after God provides this bread from heaven, the Israelites quarrel with Moses and complain that they have no water to drink. In response, God tells Moses to strike a rock, out of which water pours for the people to drink (Ex. 17:1–7). Paul sees in this episode a foreshadowing of Jesus' work, saying that all Israel "drank from the spiritual Rock that followed them, and the Rock was Christ" (1 Cor. 10:4). Indeed, although the water from this rock quenched Israel's physical thirst, it pointed to the only fount that could quench their spiritual thirst: God himself. Similarly, when passing through Samaria, Jesus told a Samaritan[1] woman that the water from Jacob's well would satisfy her physical thirst for a while, but that the living water he gives results in eternal life, quenching spiritual thirst forever (John 4:10, 14).

▶ Whole-Bible Connections

SABBATH. When God instructs Israel how to gather the manna, he tells them to gather two days' worth on the sixth day of the week so that they can honor him by resting on the seventh day (Ex. 16:22–30). Although this passage contains the first occurrence of the word "Sabbath" in Scripture (v. 23), the concept is first presented in creation when God rested on the seventh day (Gen. 2:2–3).

This divine rest in creation is later given as the grounds for Israel to rest from all their labors on the Sabbath (Ex. 20:8–11). In the New Testament, when Jesus is questioned about his actions on the seventh day, he declares that he is "lord of the Sabbath" (Matt. 12:8), and the writer of Hebrews says that those who trust in him enter God's Sabbath rest (Heb. 4:3–4).

TESTING. In these chapters, the theme of testing appears several times. When providing both sweet water and manna, God states that he is testing Israel to see if they will obey his word (Ex. 15:25–26; 16:4). However, rather than responding faithfully to God, Israel immediately quarrels with Moses and puts God to the test (17:2, 7). Psalm 95 interprets this latter testing as stemming from Israel's hard heart (Ps. 95:8–9), and the writer of Hebrews uses this Psalm to exhort his readers not to have an "evil, unbelieving heart, leading you to fall away from the living God" (Heb. 3:12).

SPIRITUAL LEADERSHIP. Jethro advises Moses to select "men who fear God, who are trustworthy and hate a bribe" to help govern the people (Ex. 18:21). These qualifications for leadership are fundamentally concerned with spiritual maturity rather than personal charisma or dynamic ability. Such spiritual requirements for leadership are later reflected in Israel's law of the king (Deut. 17:14–20) and Paul's instructions for elders and deacons (1 Tim. 3:1–13; Titus 1:5–9). In short, in order to be a good leader of God's people, one must first be a good follower of God himself.

▶ Theological Soundings

PROVIDENCE. A pervading theme throughout these chapters is God's providence. Providence simply refers to God governing his people and providing for their needs. In this section God provides his people with sweet water (Ex. 15:22–27), bread from heaven (16:1–36), and water from the rock (17:1–7). His providence is also evident in Israel's supernatural defeat of Amalek (17:8–16) and in Jethro's encounter with Moses, in which past provision of deliverance is recalled (18:1–12) and future provision of leadership is arranged (18:13–27). Significantly, the first three examples of God's providence come in response to Israel's sinful grumbling (15:24; 16:2–3; 17:3). This highlights the gracious nature of God's providence: he does not provide for his people because they are faithful, but because *he* is faithful.

SIN. This section also emphasizes Israel's sinfulness and rebellion. God's people repeatedly grumble against Moses (15:24; 16:2–3; 17:3), and even twice accuse him of seeking to kill them (16:3; 17:3). In both of these latter instances, the people's rebellion against Moses is interpreted as an affront against God himself (16:7–8; 17:2). Furthermore, Israel's disobedience to God's commands through Moses is mentioned twice in the account of the manna (16:20, 27–29), and their general lack of faith after the Red Sea deliverance stands in sharp contrast to Jethro's praise of God's supreme power based on the same event (18:9–12). These various elements combine to portray Israel as wholly sinful and unworthy recipients of God's favor.

► **Personal Implications**

Take time to reflect on the implications of Exodus 15:22–18:27 for your own life today. Make notes below on the personal implications for your walk with the Lord of the (1) *Gospel Glimpses*, (2) *Whole-Bible Connections*, (3) *Theological Soundings*, and (4) this passage as a whole.

1. Gospel Glimpses

2. Whole-Bible Connections

3. Theological Soundings

4. Exodus 15:22–18:27

As You Finish This Unit . . .

Take a moment now to ask for the Lord's blessing and help as you continue in this study of Exodus. And take a moment also to look back through this unit of study, to reflect on some key things that the Lord may be teaching you—and perhaps to highlight and underline these things to review again in the future.

Definitions

[1] **Samaritan** – A person from Samaria, which was populated with people who were part Jew and part Gentile.

WEEK 8: COVENANT LAW AT SINAI

Exodus 19:1–24:18

▲

▶ The Place of the Passage

Now that God has delivered Israel from slavery and provided for them on their journey through the wilderness, the stage is set for him to solidify his covenant relationship with them at Mount Sinai. These chapters record the giving of the law at Sinai (Ex. 20:1–23:33), surrounded by narratives describing the people's preparation for and confirmation of their covenant with God (19:1–25; 24:1–18). At both the beginning and the end, the Israelites commit themselves to living according to God's word (19:8; 24:7), and God tells them that if they are faithful to him, he will richly bless them when they enter the Promised Land (23:23–33).

▶ The Big Picture

God communicates his covenant law to Israel at Mount Sinai, and the people heartily embrace their renewed covenant relationship with him.

> ## Reflection and Discussion

Read through the whole passage for this study, Exodus 19:1–24:18. Then review the shorter passages below and write your answers to the following questions. (For further background, see the ESV Study Bible, pages 174–183; also available online at esv.org.)

1. Covenant Preparation (19:1–25)

In prefacing the law, the first thing God does is remind Israel that when he rescued them from Egypt, he brought them *to himself* (19:4). Why might this be significant for understanding the laws and requirements that follow?

In Exodus 19:9–25, how is the physical relationship between God and the people presented? What does this imply about God? What does this imply about the people?

2. Covenant Law (20:1–23:33)

In introducing the Ten Commandments, God recalls what he has done for Israel (20:2) before calling them to obey him (20:3–17). Based on this, how should we understand the role of obedience in Israel's relationship with God?

How does this parallel the role of good works in relation to the good news of Jesus?

When Jesus was asked what the most important commandment is, he said, "You shall love the Lord your God with all your heart and with all your soul and with all your mind. This is the great and first commandment. And a second is like it: You shall love your neighbor as yourself" (Matt. 22:37–39; see Deut. 6:5; Lev. 19:18). How are these two emphases—love for God and love for neighbor—reflected in the Ten Commandments?

The laws and statutes throughout these chapters are fundamentally concerned with the welfare of *others* as opposed to the welfare of *oneself* (see Ex. 20:12–17; 21:1–11, 33–36; 22:1–15, 21–27; 23:1–9). In the preceding narratives, what are some ways that Israel has been preoccupied with their own welfare, showing their need for this instruction? Inversely, how have God's actions in the preceding narratives provided examples of what it means to seek the welfare of others?

The word translated "rules" in 21:1 may also be translated "judgments." That is, the following chapters are not an exhaustive list of commands that cover every possible situation, but rather example judgments that are designed to serve as precedents and models for further legal decisions. In light of this, what quality did Israel's leaders need to govern God's people well? (For help, see 1 Kings 3:9.) How might this insight help those who lead God's people today?

Read through Exodus 21:2–11 and 22:21–23:9. How would you summarize the types of people that these laws are seeking to protect? In what ways does the concern for these types of people reflect God's heart in the gospel? (For help, see Matt. 5:3; 11:5; Luke 4:18).

The overriding concern in the laws prescribing capital punishment is respect for human life. Those who intentionally take life (Ex. 21:12–14, 18–25, 28–32) or disrespect those who gave them life (21:15, 17) are to be executed. How does Genesis 9:6 help us understand why respect for human life is so important to God? What is ultimately at issue here?

3. Covenant Confirmation (24:1–18)

The covenant is confirmed by the people promising to obey God's word (24:7), by Moses sprinkling "the blood of the covenant" on them (24:8), and by the leaders enjoying a fellowship meal in God's presence (24:9–11). How does each of these actions relate to what God says during the covenant preparation in Exodus 19:4–5?

Read through the following three sections on *Gospel Glimpses, Whole-Bible Connections,* and *Theological Soundings.* Then take time to reflect on the *Personal Implications* these sections may have for your walk with the Lord.

Gospel Glimpses

GRACE BEFORE LAW. Throughout this section, God's gracious acts on Israel's behalf consistently precede his calls for them to keep his covenant law. Before communicating his legal requirements, God twice recounts his recent deliverance of Israel from Egypt (Ex. 19:4–5; 20:2). Furthermore, God promises that his angel will pave the way for Israel to enter the Promised Land before he exhorts them to obey (23:20–21). This pattern of grace preceding law reflects the gospel, as we are saved by faith in Christ solely by God's unmerited grace, only after which, as a response to this, are we then called to obedience and good works (e.g., Eph. 2:8–10; Phil. 2:5–13).

CONCERN FOR THE OUTCAST. A core concern of the Sinai legislation is special care for the marginalized and outcast of society. Several statutes outline the rights of slaves (Ex. 21:2–11) and sojourners (22:21; 23:9), as well as widows, the fatherless (22:22–24), and the poor (23:6, 11). Similarly, in his earthly ministry Jesus displays a special concern for the outcast. He heals lepers (Matt. 8:2–3; Luke 17:12–14) and a woman who was ceremonially unclean (Matt. 9:20–22), dines with tax collectors (Matt. 9:10–13; 11:19; Luke 19:1–10), and shows compassion to prostitutes (Luke 7:36–50) and adulteresses (John 8:1–11). Such care for the marginalized is a foretaste of the personal and social wholeness that will exist when Jesus' kingdom comes in its fullness (Rev. 21:4).

THE BLOOD OF THE COVENANT. At the conclusion of the giving of the law, Moses confirms the covenant that God made with Israel by sprinkling "the blood of the covenant" on the people (Ex. 24:8). Moses, the priests, and the elders then enjoy a fellowship meal with God (24:9–11). This event prefigures the Last Supper, another divine-human meal where Jesus says that the cup is "my blood of the covenant, which is poured out for many for the forgiveness of sins" (Matt. 26:28; see also Mark 14:24).

Whole-Bible Connections

KINGDOM OF PRIESTS. God tells Israel that the whole earth belongs to him (Ex. 19:5), and that if they obey him and keep his covenant they will be for him "a kingdom of priests and a holy nation" (19:6). One of the main functions of priests was to teach people about God (see 2 Kings 17:27; 2 Chron. 15:3; Jer. 18:18). This suggests that for Israel to be a "kingdom of priests" meant that they would teach the nations about God by their faithfulness to his word. While this concept of an "international witness" is evident elsewhere in the Old Testament (e.g., Deut. 4:5–8; Isa. 51:4), it takes full form in the church's call to take the gospel to the nations. Alluding to Exodus 19:6, Peter says of the church, "But you are a chosen race, a royal priesthood, a holy nation, a people for his own possession, that you may proclaim the excellencies of him who called you out of darkness into his marvelous light" (1 Pet. 2:9).

DIVINE COMMANDMENTS. Dominating this portion of the book is God's communication of his commandments to Israel. At no point are these commandments portrayed as burdensome; rather, they are presented as clear parameters for enjoying the gracious privilege of living in relationship with a holy God. Throughout the rest of the Pentateuch[1] God will continue to reveal his will through commandments, and it was by keeping these commandments that Israel was to show their love for God (see Deut. 6:5–6; 11:1; 30:16). Although the psalmists later commend the wisdom of the law (Ps. 1:1–2; 19:7–11) and proclaim their love for it (Ps. 119:97, 113, 163), ultimately Israel's unrepentant heart prohibited them from keeping it. When Jesus came, he affirmed the continual applicability of God's commandments (Matt. 5:18–19), yet he graciously fulfilled them on our behalf (Matt. 5:17) so that we who are united to him through faith are credited with his righteousness (Rom. 5:17). Although Christians receive this righteousness solely by faith (Rom. 3:22), like Israel we too are called to show our love for God by seeking to keep his commandments (John 14:15; 1 John 5:3; 2 John 6).

Theological Soundings

THE CHARACTER OF GOD. The giving of the law at Sinai not only communicates God's will to Israel but also reveals several aspects of his character. Israel's arrival at "the mountain" (Ex. 19:2) fulfills God's promise to Moses at his call that he would "serve God on this mountain" (3:12), thereby showing God's faithfulness. The various commands to put limits between the people and the mountain reflect God's holiness (19:12, 14, 21–24). Two major concerns of the laws themselves are care for the outcast (as noted above) and the maintenance of justice within the community (e.g., in the laws prescribing punishments for causing injury [21:12–32] and restitution for loss of property [21:33–22:15]). These correlate respectively to the elements of mercy and justice that are central to God's character. Therefore, in this section, Israel is not being called to follow these commandments as an arbitrary, legalistic framework, but rather to live in a manner that is consistent with the very heart and character of God himself.

THREE USES OF THE LAW. Historically, Protestant theologians have distinguished three different uses of the law. First, the *pedagogical* use teaches us about God's righteousness and how we fall short of it. In this way the law functions to make us aware of our sin (Rom. 3:19–20). Second, the *civil* use restrains evil by prescribing punishments for wrongdoing (Deut. 13:6–11). Third, the *moral* use provides guidance for how we are to live in a way that pleases God (Matt. 5:19).

> ### Personal Implications

Take time to reflect on the implications of Exodus 19:1–24:18 for your own life today. Make notes below on the personal implications for your walk with the Lord of the (1) *Gospel Glimpses*, (2) *Whole-Bible Connections*, (3) *Theological Soundings*, and (4) this passage as a whole.

1. Gospel Glimpses

2. Whole-Bible Connections

3. Theological Soundings

4. Exodus 19:1–24:18

> ### As You Finish This Unit . . .

Take a moment now to ask for the Lord's blessing and help as you continue in this study of Exodus. And take a moment also to look back through this unit of study, to reflect on some key things that the Lord may be teaching you—and perhaps to highlight and underline these things to review again in the future.

Definitions

[1] **Pentateuch** – The first five books of the Bible.

Week 9: Instructions for Building the Tabernacle

Exodus 25:1–31:18

The Place of the Passage

After rescuing his people (Exodus 1–18) and communicating his covenant law to them (Exodus 19–24), in these chapters God instructs Israel how to receive his holy presence in their midst. The tabernacle and all of its furnishings (chs. 25–27, 30) provide the space for God's special presence to dwell with his people, and the craftsmen and priests (chs. 28–29, 31) serve at the tabernacle by building it and ministering in it. The instructions provided in these chapters will soon see their realization in chapters 35–40, where God graciously comes to dwell in the midst of his people.

The Big Picture

God instructs Israel how to build the tabernacle and consecrate the priests, providing the structure and servants needed for him to dwell with his people.

> ### Reflection and Discussion

Read through the whole passage for this study, Exodus 25:1–31:18. Then review the shorter passages below and write your answers to the following questions. (For further background, see the *ESV Study Bible*, pages 183–196; also available online at esv.org.)

1. The Items of the Tabernacle (chs. 25–27, 30)

The tabernacle is furnished by contributions from the people, from "every man whose heart moves him" (Ex. 25:2). In the previous narratives, what was the ultimate source of the people's wealth from which these contributions are given (see 3:21; 12:35–36)? What might this teach us about our own wealth and how God builds his church today?

Repeatedly God commands that the tabernacle and its furnishings be made according to the pattern that he reveals (Ex. 25:9, 40; 27:8). How do Hebrews 8:1–5 and 9:11–12 help us understand the significance of these statements for the Christian?

The first item to be constructed for the tabernacle is the ark of the covenant (Ex. 25:10–16). According to Numbers 10:35; 1 Samuel 4:1–8; and Psalm 132:8, what is the significance of the ark? What does this reveal about the function of the tabernacle?

Two cherubim are built above the mercy seat that rests upon the ark (Ex. 25:17–21). The only other time cherubim have been mentioned in Scripture is in Genesis 3:24, when cherubim were stationed at the edge of the garden to keep banished humanity away from God's presence and from accessing the tree of life. In light of this, how is the grace of God revealed in the reappearance of the cherubim here?

A veil separates the Most Holy Place from the Holy Place (Ex. 26:33), partitioning God's presence from the outside world. How does this shed light on the significance of what happens in Matthew 27:51 upon Jesus' death?

2. The People of the Tabernacle (chs. 28–29, 31)

The shoulder piece of the priest's ephod has two onyx stones with the names of six tribes inscribed on each (28:9–12), and the breastpiece has 12 stones, each representing one of the 12 tribes (28:17–21). By wearing these garments, Aaron represents God's people as he enters before the Lord (28:29). In what way does this foreshadow the work of Jesus? (For help, see Rom. 8:33–34; Heb. 7:23–25.)

In consecrating Aaron and his sons for their priestly service, the first sacrifice required is a bull for a sin offering (Ex. 29:10–14). Read Leviticus 4:3. What does the need of a sin offering imply about Aaron and his sons? What are some implications of this for their priestly ministry?

In the closing section (31:12–17), God commands Israel three times to keep the Sabbath. What are the reasons given for Israel to do this?

Read through the following three sections on *Gospel Glimpses*, *Whole-Bible Connections*, and *Theological Soundings*. Then take time to reflect on the *Personal Implications* these sections may have for your walk with the Lord.

▶ Gospel Glimpses

PRIESTLY SACRIFICES. The consecration of the priests involves multiple sacrifices. Three times Aaron and his sons must lay their hands on a sacrifice, symbolically transferring their guilt to the animal (Ex. 29:10, 15, 19). The first two of these sacrifices are a sin offering (29:14) and a burnt offering (29:18), both of which are later described as atoning for sin (Lev. 4:20; 1:3–4, respectively). Only after these sacrifices are made are the priests considered holy (Ex. 29:21). The priests are later instructed to offer daily sacrifices on the altar, once in the morning and once in the evening (Ex. 29:38–39). This need for the priests to make atonement for themselves and then perpetually offer sacrifices for the people shows the inherent limitation of their ministry and points forward to Jesus' sacrificial work on the cross. Unlike these Old Testament priests, Jesus needs neither to make atonement for himself nor to offer himself perpetually for his people—his once-for-all sacrificial death brings full and final salvation for all those who trust him (see Heb. 7:26–28; 10:14).

GOD THE HEAVENLY KING. In these chapters the tabernacle is presented as a mobile palace, with God portrayed as the heavenly king. The ark serves as God's footstool (1 Chron. 28:2), above which his heavenly throne symbolically sits (Isa. 66:1). The blue and purple yarns of the curtains (Ex. 26:1) and veil (Ex. 26:31) represent heaven and royalty, respectively, and the cherubim that are above the ark (Ex. 25:18) and worked into the tapestries (Ex. 26:1, 31) depict the tabernacle as a heavenly structure. This portrayal of God as the heavenly king forms the background to the preaching of John the Baptist and Jesus, who both begin their ministries by saying, "Repent, for *the kingdom of heaven* is at hand" (Matt. 3:2; 4:17). That is, Jesus, whose "kingdom is not of this world" (John 18:36), has come to save his people and bring them into his heavenly kingdom (Luke 23:42–43).

▶ Whole-Bible Connections

TWELVE STONES/TRIBES. The 12 stones on Aaron's breastpiece represent the 12 tribes of Israel (Ex. 28:17–21). Just as God's people consist of 12 tribes in the Old Testament, stemming from the 12 sons of Israel (Ex. 1:1–7), so do God's people in the New Testament era stem from the 12 apostles of Christ (Eph. 2:19–20). In John's final vision of the New Jerusalem, the gates of the eternal city have the names of the 12 tribes of Israel inscribed (Rev. 21:12), while the foundations of the city wall have the names of the 12 apostles (Rev. 21:14). These foundations are also adorned with 12 stones that correspond to the 12 stones of the priestly breastpiece (Rev. 21:19–20). Therefore, just as Aaron represented God's people as he entered God's presence in the tabernacle, so do the gates and foundations of the New Jerusalem show that all of God's people—both old covenant and new covenant—will dwell in his presence forever.

A NEW EDEN. In various ways the tabernacle is presented as a new Eden. Since the tabernacle faces east (Ex. 27:13–16; Num. 3:38), the cherubim woven into the veil of the Most Holy Place (Ex. 26:31) recall the cherubim stationed on the east side of the garden of Eden (Gen. 3:24). The lampstand (Ex. 25:31–40) represents the tree of life (Gen. 2:9), and the terms used to describe Adam "working" and "keeping" the garden (Gen. 2:15) are used together elsewhere to describe the Levites' service at the tabernacle (Num. 3:7–8; 8:26; 18:7). Even the three-part structure of the tabernacle (Most Holy Place, Holy Place, outer court) corresponds to the three sections of creation (garden, land of Eden, remainder of creation). Creation imagery is later present in Ezekiel's vision of a restored temple, which like Eden faces east (Ezek. 47:1), has water flowing out from it (Ezek. 47:1; Gen. 2:10), and is full of trees (Ezek. 47:7; Gen. 2:9). These themes are picked up finally in John's vision of the New Jerusalem, which similarly has water flowing out from it (Rev. 22:1) and is surrounded by the tree of life (Rev. 22:2).

▶ Theological Soundings

WORSHIP. Virtually every aspect of these chapters relates to the theme of worship. The tabernacle is the central location of Israelite worship (Exodus 26); the various items within the tabernacle are all used in worship (chs. 25, 27, 30); the priests are those who minister on behalf of the people during worship (chs. 28–29); and the Sabbath was a day when certain special worship-related activities occurred (Exodus 31; see Lev. 24:8; Num. 28:9–10; 1 Chron. 9:32; 2 Chron. 23:8). The detailed instructions throughout these chapters show that God desires his people to worship him according to his specifications. However, other passages reveal that God is not pleased with worship that is formally correct if one's lifestyle does not reflect a heart of faith (Isa. 1:11–17; Amos 5:21–24; Mic. 6:6–8). Conversely, Scripture presents God as graciously willing to accept worship that is externally incorrect if one's heart is set on seeking him (2 Chron. 30:18–20).

ATONEMENT. These chapters contain the first instructions in Scripture concerning atonement. The sin offering is first mentioned here (Ex. 29:14, 36; 30:10), which according to Leviticus is a means by which a person who sins can be atoned for (Lev. 4:20, 26, 31, 35). Significantly, these verses in Leviticus all state that when atonement is made for someone, forgiveness follows. Since the New Testament describes Jesus' death as a sin offering (Heb. 13:11–12), it follows that those for whom he died and made atonement receive God's forgiveness (Eph. 1:7; Col. 1:14).

Personal Implications

Take time to reflect on the implications of Exodus 25:1–31:18 for your own life today. Make notes below on the personal implications for your walk with the Lord of the (1) *Gospel Glimpses*, (2) *Whole-Bible Connections*, (3) *Theological Soundings*, and (4) this passage as a whole.

1. Gospel Glimpses

2. Whole-Bible Connections

3. Theological Soundings

4. Exodus 25:1–31:18

As You Finish This Unit . . .

Take a moment now to ask for the Lord's blessing and help as you continue in this study of Exodus. And take a moment also to look back through this unit of study, to reflect on some key things that the Lord may be teaching you—and perhaps to highlight and underline these things to review again in the future.

WEEK 10: COVENANT VIOLATION, INTERCESSION, AND RENEWAL

Exodus 32:1–34:35

The Place of the Passage

When God brought Israel to Mount Sinai, he communicated his covenant law to them (chs. 19–24) and showed Moses how to construct the tabernacle, which would provide a place for him to dwell among his people (chs. 25–31). In the present section, before Moses comes down the mountain, Israel breaks God's law and thus jeopardizes their right to have him dwell with them. After Moses intercedes for the people, God graciously forgives their sin and reconfirms his covenant with them, thereby opening the way for Israel to build the tabernacle and enjoy God's presence (chs. 35–40).

The Big Picture

Israel breaks God's covenant law, but Moses intercedes for them and God graciously renews his covenant with them.

75

> ### Reflection and Discussion

Read through the whole passage for this study, Exodus 32:1–34:35. Then review the shorter passages below and write your answers to the following questions. (For further background, see the *ESV Study Bible*, pages 196–201; also available online at esv.org.)

1. Covenant Violation (32:1–35)

In this section, the people's covenant violation is presented as a distorted version of their covenant ceremony with God from chapters 19–24. In 32:1–6, which of God's commands do they break? What other aspects from the earlier covenant ceremony are alluded to here? (For help, see Ex. 20:2; 24:3–11.)

In response to the people's violation, God decides to destroy them and start over with Moses (32:7–10), but Moses intercedes and God relents (vv. 11–14). What are the two main reasons Moses gives for why God should relent? What is Moses primarily concerned with in this act of intercession?

Moses and Aaron are sharply contrasted in this chapter. First, whereas Moses led the people in the true covenant ceremony of chapters 19–24, here Aaron leads them in a mutated version, in 32:1–6. Second, Moses is singled out by God as the one to continue the covenant people (32:10), while Aaron is singled out twice as the one who allowed the covenant people to go astray (32:25, 35). Third, while Moses uses fire to destroy Israel's idol (32:20), Aaron claims that it was the fire that produced the idol (32:24). These contrasts highlight Moses' faithful role as Israel's mediator in this chapter. In what ways do Moses' actions here foreshadow the work of Jesus?

2. Covenant Intercession (33:1–23)

Biblical writers often repeat information to emphasize a point. What information is repeated in Exodus 33:1–6? Given the flow of Exodus, why is this such a devastating problem? See Exodus 3:12; 19:4; 25:8 for further insight.

What information is repeated (three times!) in Exodus 33:7? How does this add to the tension introduced in the previous verses?

After Moses intercedes for Israel again (Ex. 33:12–16), God agrees to accompany them, despite their shocking lapse (v. 17). In response, Moses says, "Please show me your glory" (v. 18). In light of Exodus 24:15–17 and 29:43–46, why is Moses asking to see God's glory here?

In response to Moses' request, God says that he will make all his goodness pass before Moses and proclaim his name, "The LORD" (33:19). Given the tension introduced in 33:1–6, what is the significance of God proclaiming his name here? (For help, review the discussion of "God's Name" in Week 3.)

3. Covenant Renewal (34:1–35)

When Israel broke the covenant in chapter 32, Moses broke the tablets that had the covenant law written on them (32:19). In light of this, what is significant about God's command to Moses in 34:1?

To confirm his forgiveness of Israel and his intent to continue on with them, God passes by Moses and proclaims his name (Ex. 34:5–7). What aspects of God's character does this name proclamation focus on? What does this suggest is the grounds for God's forgiveness of Israel and his determination to move forward with them?

After God reconfirms the covenant by reiterating various commands (34:10–28), this section ends by noting how Moses' face would shine after he would enter God's presence to speak with him (vv. 29–35). The apostle Paul notes that it was God's "glory" that caused Moses' face to shine in this way (2 Cor. 3:7).

Given the significance of God's "glory" in this section, how is this a fitting resolution to this section of the book?

Read through the following three sections on *Gospel Glimpses, Whole-Bible Connections*, and *Theological Soundings*. Then take time to reflect on the *Personal Implications* these sections may have for your walk with the Lord.

Gospel Glimpses

GRACE FOR FAILURES. Shortly after committing themselves to obeying God's law (Ex. 24:7), in this passage the Israelites show themselves to be wholesale failures at covenant keeping. By desiring other gods (32:1) and making an idol for themselves (32:4), they directly violate the first two commandments (20:3–4). However, despite this failure, God forgives his people based on Moses' intercession and his own abounding grace. In interceding for the people and requesting God's continued presence with them, Moses appeals five times for God's "favor" (33:12, 13 [2x], 16; 34:9), which may also be translated as "grace." God responds to this by reaffirming his intent to accompany Israel based on his "favor" (33:17) and by reconfirming his covenant relationship with them (34:10–28). In short, God forgives his people's failures not because they get their act together, but because of his gracious and merciful character (see 33:19).

BEHOLDING GOD WITH UNVEILED FACES. When Moses descends the mountain, and anytime afterward when he speaks with God, his face shines brightly because of God's glory (Ex. 34:29–35). Moses would veil his face when he left God's presence, and he would remove the veil when he entered to speak with God again. Paul uses this passage to contrast the greater glory that Christians behold in the new covenant with Christ. Although the old covenant was glorious, it was limited because it did not enable the people to keep it. Paul says that "their minds were hardened" (2 Cor. 3:14), describing this as a veil lying over their hearts (v. 15). However, through Christ "the veil is removed" (v. 16) and we are able to behold God's glory. The astounding news of the gospel is that this "veil lifting" through Christ is not accomplished by our own efforts, but by the transforming work of God's Spirit (v. 18).

> ## Whole-Bible Connections

STIFF-NECKED PEOPLE. Four times in this passage Israel is referred to as a "stiff-necked" people (Ex. 32:9; 33:3, 5; 34:9), reflecting the fact that they are inclined toward disobedience and impenitence. After the fall, humanity's natural inclination has always been to rebel against God and not submit to his ways. During Noah's time, every inclination of people's hearts was "only evil continually" (Gen. 6:5). Later on, Moses foretells that Israel will continue in their rebellion after he dies (Deut. 31:27, 29), something that ultimately leads to their exile from the Promised Land (2 Kings 17:13–20; Neh. 9:29–30). In exile, the prophet Ezekiel is told that his audience will not listen to him because they have a "hard forehead and a stubborn heart" (Ezek. 3:7). In the New Testament, shortly after recalling the golden calf incident, Stephen calls his accusers "stiff-necked people," saying that they "always resist the Holy Spirit" (Acts 7:51). Ultimately, this "stiff-necked" posture is due to fallen humanity's unwillingness and incapability to submit to God's law (Rom. 8:7), and the only cure for this condition is the gracious work of God's Spirit giving us new life (Rom. 8:9–11).

THE NAME OF THE LORD. When God passes by Moses to proclaim his "name," he gives him a full-length description of himself, focusing on his merciful, gracious, patient, and faithful character (Ex. 34:6–7). This self-description becomes a confession[1] of faith concerning God's character throughout the Old Testament. Several psalms recall this statement (Ps. 86:15; 103:8; 145:8), as do Joel (2:13), Jonah (4:2), and Nehemiah (9:17). The opening of John's gospel also alludes to this proclamation of God's name. After noting that the Word became flesh and dwelt among us, John says, "we have seen his glory, glory as of the only Son from the Father, *full of grace and truth*" (John 1:14). The first phrase recalls Moses' request to see God's glory (Ex. 33:18, 22), and the last is very similar to the end of Exodus 34:6, "abounding in steadfast love and faithfulness." This shows that the character of God evident in the Old Testament finds its fullest expression in the person of Jesus Christ.

> ## Theological Soundings

IDOLATRY. The core issue in the rebellion at Mount Sinai is idolatry. Simply defined, idolatry occurs when we put something else in the place of God in our lives. In the case of Israel, they fashion a golden calf and credit it with God's deliverance of them from Egypt (Ex. 32:4; compare 20:2). Then they mimic the covenant confirmation ceremony with God from chapter 24 by rising early in the morning, offering burnt and peace offerings, and eating and drinking (32:6; compare 24:4–5, 11). Paul cites this golden calf incident and encourages his Christian readers to learn from Israel's errors and not be idolaters as they were (1 Cor. 10:7). However, idolatry is not limited to worshiping golden statues. God later condemns Israel for having taken "idols into their hearts" (Ezek. 14:3), revealing that anything we exalt above God—whether a statue or a desire of the heart—can fittingly be called an idol.

INTERCESSION. The catalyst for God's forgiveness of the people in this section is Moses' intercession. Four times in these chapters Moses intercedes for Israel, asking God to forgive their sin and continue to accompany them to the Promised Land (Ex. 32:11–14, 31–32; 33:12–16; 34:9). This focus on intercession that leads to forgiveness ultimately highlights God's merciful heart: he is willing to forgive his people who have gone astray based on the appeals of another. This theological truth is shown forth most clearly through the intercessory work of Jesus. Because Jesus stands before God and thereby intercedes for his people, no one has grounds to condemn them (Rom. 8:34) and they are saved "to the uttermost" (Heb. 7:25).

▶ Personal Implications

Take time to reflect on the implications of Exodus 32:1–34:35 for your own life today. Make notes below on the personal implications for your walk with the Lord of the (1) *Gospel Glimpses*, (2) *Whole-Bible Connections*, (3) *Theological Soundings*, and (4) this passage as a whole.

1. Gospel Glimpses

2. Whole-Bible Connections

3. Theological Soundings

4. Exodus 32:1–34:35

► As You Finish This Unit . . .

Take a moment now to ask for the Lord's blessing and help as you continue in this study of Exodus. And take a moment also to look back through this unit of study, to reflect on some key things that the Lord may be teaching you—and perhaps to highlight and underline these things to review again in the future.

Definitions

[1] **Confession** – Public acknowledgment of belief (2 Cor. 9:13; Heb. 4:14) or of sin (Ezra 10:1; James 5:16; 1 John 1:9).

WEEK 11: CONSTRUCTION OF THE TABERNACLE

Exodus 35:1–40:38

The Place of the Passage

The book of Exodus concludes with the construction of the tabernacle. In response to God's detailed instructions, outlined in chapters 25–31, the people obediently build the tabernacle. After the tabernacle is built and assembled, the section ends with God descending upon it through his glory cloud as he comes to dwell in the midst of his people. Whereas Exodus began with Israel enslaved in the midst of Egypt, it ends with God enthroned in the midst of Israel.

The Big Picture

Israel builds the tabernacle according to God's instructions, and God comes to live in their midst.

> ### Reflection and Discussion

Read through the whole passage for this study, Exodus 35:1–40:38. Then review the shorter passages below and write your answers to the following questions. (For further background, see the *ESV Study Bible*, pages 201–209; also available online at esv.org.)

1. Tabernacle Preparation (35:1–36:7)

The instructions for building the tabernacle end with a command to rest from work on the Sabbath (31:12–17), a theme that is reiterated here at the beginning of the tabernacle's construction (35:1–3). What do these Sabbath commands teach us about Israel's responsibility as they undertake this work of building the tabernacle? How does the account between the Sabbath commands (chs. 32–34) reinforce this?

In Exodus 35:20–29, the people respond to Moses' call for contributions for the construction of the tabernacle. How are the people repeatedly described throughout these verses? What does this teach us about the nature of true obedience?

According to Exodus 35:30–36:1, how did Bezalel and Oholiab acquire their skills and knowledge? What does this suggest about our own skills and knowledge? What attitude(s) should this instill in us concerning our personal abilities?

----

2. Tabernacle Construction (36:8–39:43)

These chapters describe in detail the fulfillment of the tabernacle instructions from chapters 25–30, as the following table summarizes:

	Instructions	Fulfillment
Tabernacle Proper	26:1–37	36:8–38
Ark	25:10–22	37:1–9
Table	25:23–30	37:10–16
Lampstand	25:31–40	37:17–24
Altar of Incense	30:1–10	37:25–28
Anointing Oil and Incense	30:22–38	37:29
Altar of Burnt Offering	27:1–8	38:1–7
Bronze Basin	30:17–21	38:8
Court	27:9–19	38:9–20
Priestly Garments	28:1–43	39:1–31

Why would Moses spend so much time describing the fulfillment of all these detailed instructions concerning the tabernacle? What does this emphasize about the people's response to God's word? (For help, review Ex. 25:9.)

How does Exodus 39:32–43 support the above observation? How might this challenge/encourage us today?

----

3. Tabernacle Assembly (40:1–33)

After the tabernacle is constructed, God commands Moses to anoint[1] it "so that it may become holy" (40:9). Before this in Exodus, only one location has been described as holy: Mount Sinai (3:5; 19:23). Significantly, both of these verses describing God's presence at Sinai emphasize the *distance* required between God and his people. However, through the tabernacle God brings his holy presence *right into the midst* of his people. In what ways does this foreshadow the gospel?

After God's glory cloud fills the tabernacle (40:34–35), the final verses of the book describe how God leads Israel throughout all their journeys (vv. 36–38). What might be considered a New Testament counterpart to this idea of God accompanying his people as they journey? (For help, see John 14:15–17.)

Read through the following three sections on *Gospel Glimpses*, *Whole-Bible Connections*, and *Theological Soundings*. Then take time to reflect on the *Personal Implications* these sections may have for your walk with the Lord.

Gospel Glimpses

THE MERCY SEAT. One of the central features of the tabernacle is the mercy seat (Ex. 35:12; 37:6–9; 39:35; 40:20). Once a year, on the Day of Atonement, the high priest was allowed to enter the Most Holy Place. On this day he would take the blood of a sin offering and sprinkle it on the mercy seat to make atonement for the sins of the whole nation (Lev. 16:15). This great act at the mercy seat prefigures the saving work of Jesus on the cross. The New Testament not only describes Jesus as a high priest who enters the Most Holy Place and sprinkles his own blood (Heb. 9:11–14), but it may also describe him *as the mercy seat itself.* Paul says that redemption comes through Jesus, "whom God put forward as a propitiation" (Rom. 3:25). The word "propitiation" here translates the Greek equivalent of the Hebrew word for "mercy seat," which may be what Paul had in mind. That is, while atonement under the old covenant was made at the mercy seat, atonement under the new covenant is made through Jesus.

GOD WITH US. A precious truth of the gospel is that not only does God save us by his grace, but he also comes to live with us. This truth is evident in the story of the exodus, as God saves his people from Egypt (Exodus 1–18) and then comes to live with them in the tabernacle (chs. 35–40). This connection between salvation and divine presence is summarized earlier in Exodus 29:46: "And they shall know that I am the LORD their God, who brought them out of the land of Egypt that I might dwell among them." These two gospel elements—salvation and presence—are also reflected in the names given to Christ at his birth. According to Matthew's gospel, when Christ is born, he is called Jesus, "for he will save his people from their sins" (Matt. 1:21), and also Immanuel, "which means, God with us" (Matt. 1:23).

Whole-Bible Connections

HEART-FELT GENEROSITY. The Israelites are portrayed in these chapters as exceedingly generous in their giving toward the construction of the tabernacle. Moses calls for all those who have a "generous heart" (Ex. 35:5) to contribute toward the work, and the description of the people giving repeatedly focuses on the "heart" of those participating (35:21, 22, 26, 29). In the end, the people give so much that Moses tells them to stop because the craftsmen have more material than they need (36:3–7)! Such heartfelt generosity is extolled throughout the Old Testament in the law (Deut. 15:10–11; 24:19–22), the historical books (1 Chron. 29:6–9), and the poetic books (Ps. 37:21, 26; 112:5; Prov. 11:25; 22:9), as well as in the New Testament (Matt. 19:21; Acts 10:1–2; Rom. 12:8; 1 Tim. 6:17–18). Perhaps best representing this theme is Paul's call for the Corinthian believers to give freely toward a relief fund for the Jerusalem church. He says, "Each one must give as he has decided in his heart, not reluctantly or under compulsion, for God loves a cheerful giver" (2 Cor. 9:7).

MOST HOLY PLACE. At the center of the tabernacle, behind the innermost veil, is the Most Holy Place (Ex. 40:3; see also 26:33–34). This inner sanctuary houses the ark of the covenant, which represents God's kingly presence on earth (see e.g., 1 Sam. 4:4; Ps. 99:1; Isa. 37:16). When Solomon later constructs the temple, the Most Holy Place becomes established more permanently in Israel's midst (1 Kings 8:6), thereby providing a longstanding place for God to reside with his people. However, after centuries of Israel living in unrepented sin, God departs the Most Holy Place in judgment (Ezek. 10:18–19; 11:22–23). When Jesus died on the cross, the veil to the Most Holy Place was torn in two (Matt. 27:51), showing that the barrier between God's presence and his people had been removed. Finally, in Revelation, John pictures the New Jerusalem as cubic in shape (Rev. 21:16), which recalls the cubic shape of the Most Holy Place (1 Kings 6:20). This reveals that the eternal home of believers will be a worldwide Most Holy Place—God's kingly presence will be everywhere.

> ## Theological Soundings

SPIRITUAL GIFTS. God provides his people with various skills and abilities to enable them to serve him and others. These are known as "spiritual gifts" (see 1 Cor. 12:1–11). This is evident in this section as God calls Bezalel and Oholiab to build the tabernacle, fills them with his Spirit, and gives them the skills and knowledge necessary to carry out the task (Ex. 35:30–35; 36:1–2; 38:22–23). From other Scripture we see that God gives each of his people at least one spiritual gift (Eph. 4:7–8; 1 Pet. 4:10), that people are often gifted differently from each other (Rom. 12:4–8; 1 Cor. 12:4–11, 28; Eph. 4:11–12), that all of these different gifts are important (1 Cor. 12:12–27), and that all spiritual gifts should be used to build up the body of Christ (1 Cor. 12:7; Eph. 4:11–12; 1 Pet. 4:10).

FAITH AND OBEDIENCE. One of the precious truths of the gospel is that we are saved by grace through faith, which is "not a result of works" (Eph. 2:8–9). However, it is also true that through this gracious salvation we are "created in Christ Jesus for good works" (Eph. 2:10). That is, although our obedience to God's word does not save us, it is evidence that we have been saved. Illustrating this, at the conclusion of the tabernacle construction the text repeatedly emphasizes that the people had responded obediently to God's word through Moses (Ex. 39:32, 42–43). This obedient response was evidence that the people believed Moses (see 19:9), and therefore that they believed God (19:7–8). Having been graciously saved through the exodus, their faith was then demonstrated by their works (see James 2:18).

Personal Implications

Take time to reflect on the implications of Exodus 35:1–40:38 for your own life today. Make notes below on the personal implications for your walk with the Lord of the (1) *Gospel Glimpses*, (2) *Whole-Bible Connections*, (3) *Theological Soundings*, and (4) this passage as a whole.

1. Gospel Glimpses

2. Whole-Bible Connections

3. Theological Soundings

4. Exodus 35:1–40:38

As You Finish This Unit . . .

Take a moment now to ask for the Lord's blessing and help as you continue in this study of Exodus. And take a moment also to look back through this unit of study, to reflect on some key things that the Lord may be teaching you—and perhaps to highlight and underline these things to review again in the future.

Definitions

[1] **Anoint** – In Scripture, to pour oil (usually olive oil) on someone or something to set the person or thing apart for a special purpose.

WEEK 12: SUMMARY AND CONCLUSION

▲

As we conclude this study of Exodus, we begin by summarizing the big picture of the book as a whole. We will then review some questions for reflection in light of the entire Exodus account, with a final identification of Gospel Glimpses, Whole-Bible Connections, and Theological Soundings, all with a view to appreciating the book of Exodus in its entirety.

▶ The Big Picture of Exodus

Over the course of this study we have seen that Exodus divides into two major parts.

The first part (Ex. 1:1–18:27) records Israel's exodus from Egypt. God calls Moses to lead Israel out of their oppressive situation in Egypt, sends plagues against the Egyptians, delivers Israel at the Red Sea, and then guides them through the wilderness to the foot of Mount Sinai.

The second part (19:1–40:38) details the covenant God made with Israel at Mount Sinai. As a response to God's gracious salvation through the exodus, Israel is called to commit themselves to living according to God's word. After receiving God's covenant law and instructions for building the tabernacle,

Israel violates the covenant by their idolatry of the golden calf. Once again, however, God shows himself to be gracious and forgives their sin. Israel then responds faithfully to God's word by constructing the tabernacle according to his specifications, after which he comes to dwell in their midst.

Putting both of these parts together, the book of Exodus shows us that the God of Israel graciously saves his people, forgives their sin, and pursues relationship with them. This basic storyline provides a marvelous foretaste of the gospel of Jesus Christ. Through Jesus' life, death, and resurrection, God has fully and finally saved his people by his grace. Because of Jesus' work on our behalf, we are forgiven in God's sight, and through the outpouring of the Holy Spirit God has come to live in our midst. (For further background, see the ESV Study Bible, pages 139–144; also online at esv.org.)

Read through the following three sections on *Gospel Glimpses, Whole-Bible Connections*, and *Theological Soundings*. Then take time to reflect on the *Personal Implications* these sections may have for your walk with the Lord.

▶ Gospel Glimpses

Throughout the book of Exodus we have seen many instances where God's grace is evident and the gospel is reflected. God saw his people in misery and suffering, and due to his compassion and covenant commitment he responded by saving them. He showed his power through the plagues and his mercy through the Passover, and despite Israel's doubts and grumbling as he delivered them, God continued to provide for them along the way. God's grace was the foundation upon which the law was given, and his mercy was demonstrated after Israel quickly violated that law. In the end, Israel experienced God's gracious presence as he descended upon the tabernacle and came to live in their midst.

Has your understanding of the gospel changed at all during the course of this study? If so, how?

Are there any particular passages in Exodus that have brought the gospel home to you in a fresh way?

▶ Whole-Bible Connections

Many images and events from Exodus are recalled and echoed throughout the rest of Scripture. For example, Israel's fruitfulness and multiplication (Ex. 1:7) alludes back to God's original mandate to Adam at creation (Gen. 1:28) and finds its fullest expression in the spread of the gospel through the church (Acts 6:7; 12:24). In addition, images such as God as the divine warrior, Israel as a kingdom of priests, and the tabernacle as a new Eden are all elaborated upon as the storyline of the Bible unfolds. In fact, the story of Exodus itself is a microcosm[1] of the overall story of Scripture: God sees his people in need, saves them by his grace, and comes to live in their midst.

How has your understanding of the place of Exodus in the sweep of the Bible been deepened through your study of Exodus?

What are some connections in Exodus to the New Testament that you hadn't noticed before?

Has your understanding of the unity of the Bible been clarified through studying Exodus? How so?

What development has there been in your view of how the Old Testament prefigures the person and work of Jesus?

> **Theological Soundings**

Exodus contributes much to Christian theology. Doctrines that are addressed and reinforced include God's sovereignty, election, substitution, providence, sin, atonement, idolatry, and spiritual gifts.

Where has your theology been tweaked or corrected as you have studied Exodus?

How might our understanding of God be impoverished if we did not have the book of Exodus?

How does Exodus uniquely contribute to and clarify our understanding of Jesus?

Are there any specific ways in which Exodus helps us understand the human condition?

Personal Implications

As you consider the book of Exodus as a whole, what implications do you see for your own life? Consider especially the relationship between God's grace and his call for his people to obey him. What are the ramifications for your own life of Exodus's teaching on what it means to be a follower of God?

What implications for life flow from your reflections on the questions already asked in this week's study concerning Gospel Glimpses, Whole-Bible Connections, and Theological Soundings?

What have you learned in Exodus that might lead you to praise God, turn away from sin, or trust more firmly in his promises?

As You Finish Studying Exodus . . .

We rejoice with you as you finish studying the book of Exodus! May this study become part of your Christian walk of faith, day-by-day and week-by-week throughout all your life. Now we would greatly encourage you to continue to study the Word of God on a week-by-week basis. To continue your study of the Bible, we would encourage you to consider other books in the *Knowing the Bible* series, and to visit www.knowingthebibleseries.org.

Lastly, take a moment to look back through this study. Review again the notes that you have written, and the things that you have highlighted or underlined. Reflect again on the key themes that the Lord has been teaching you about himself and about his Word. May these things become a treasure for you throughout your life—this we pray in the name of the Father, and the Son, and the Holy Spirit. Amen.

Definitions

[1] **Microcosm** – A small version of a larger reality (literally, a "small world").